Life as Worship: PRAYER AND PRAISE IN JESUS' NAME

by THEODORE W. JENNINGS, JR.

WM. B. EERDMANS PUBL. CO., GRAND RAPIDS

MARSHALL, MORGAN & SCOTT PUBL. LTD., LONDON

Printed in the United States of America
for
Wm. B. Eerdmans Publishing Co.
255 Jefferson Ave., S.E., Grand Rapids, MI 49503
and
Marshall, Morgan & Scott
Bath Street, London ECIV9LB

ISBN 0 551 01017 7

We gratefully acknowledge permission to use "My prayers must
meet a brazen heaven" by Gerard Manley Hopkins, found in the
fourth edition of *The Poems of Gerard Manley Hopkins*, ed. W. H.
Gardner and N. H. MacKenzie (New York: Oxford University Press,
1967).

Library of Congress Cataloging in Publication Data

Jennings, Theodore W.
  Life as worship.

  1. Prayer. 2. Praise of God. I. Title.
BV210.2.J46 1982   248.3'2   82-7283
ISBN 0-8028-1913-3   AACR2

For Robert, Steve, and Richard
   whose lives were prayers for liberation
   whose voices have been silenced
   whose prayers will yet be heard

and for Ronna
   who asked me about prayer
   who taught me about singing
     with thanksgiving

CONTENTS

Preface

Today a gulf separates the work of theology and the life of the Christian community. Two principal factors have created this division. First, in order to meet the standards (real or imagined) of academic study, theology has had to preoccupy itself with questions of method and presuppositions to such a degree that the actual work of interpreting the Christian faith seems endlessly deferred or postponed. Second, the Christian community has become preoccupied with questions of institutional extension or preservation, leaving little time or energy for the study of its Christian character. The result is that theology as a reflection upon the basic character of Christian faith seems almost to have disappeared, while the community of faith has become like a social institution whose specifically Christian identity is simply assumed but seldom made evident.

In order to overcome this situation, we cannot simply "translate" theological statements into the popular jargon of the institution; a dialogue between sterile theory and blind practice can produce nothing of value. If this stalemate is to be broken, theology must begin with the practice of the community. We must begin with the activity that makes this community Christian—with worship. From this point it will be possible to ask about the theological meaning of this action and its meaning for our life, and therefore for all we do.

We do a great many things when we worship: we preach and read scripture, we confess our sins and receive assurance and absolution, we break bread and drink wine, we baptize, we celebrate marriages and mourn deaths, we pray and we sing praise. That we do these things and the way that we do them makes it clear that we are the Christian community. Obviously, this book cannot address all of these actions. As the title makes plain, *Life as Worship* is about prayer and praise. Perhaps other books will follow this one and address the other actions of worship.

If you ask me how I came to write a book about prayer, all I can do is recount the events that led up to it. Like most children raised in a Christian home, I asked some difficult questions about prayer. My parents and my teachers gave me good answers, but because I was working toward becoming a theologian, I didn't stop asking questions. Then the time came when others asked me about prayer. I don't know if they were satisfied with my answers, but I wasn't, and neither was the minister I married. She taught me to ask the right questions and helped me to keep asking them.

My first lectures on prayer were given for clergy living in and around Memphis, Tennessee, at the request of the Reverend Michael Ripski, who also prepared transcripts of those lectures. They were subsequently expanded for the Course of Study School at Candler School of Theology. Aided by the responses of both of these groups to these lectures, I was able to formulate my ideas more clearly, and felt encouraged to write this book.

Four people read the manuscript and made many useful suggestions: Professor James W. May (who first taught me about public prayer), Professor Charles D. Hackett, Professor Manfred Hoffman, and Professor Don E. Saliers, all of the Candler School of Theology. It was typed by Susan Ashworth and Helen Patton. I am grateful to them and for them.

In writing this book I have had the situation of the church continually in mind. It was during a sabbatical in South Africa that the importance of a theology *for* the church was brought home to me—especially through my association with the now "banned" Christian Institute. It was through this group of Christians, committed to witness to the single lordship of Christ, that I came to know the three men to whom this book is dedicated. I do not know in what manner these three prayed; as is true also for us, that must remain their secret. But the world knows for what they lived and in what circumstances they died. Through their lives the cry for justice was sounded—a cry that will not be silenced until all is transformed.

Finally, this book is also dedicated to one without whom it would never have occurred to me to write about prayer. She works in a hospital, accompanying the gravely ill on their journeys into the valley of the shadow of death. Yet to her is given a song that awakens courage in the night and joy in the dawn. In sharing with me both her life and her song, she has been "neighbor to this man."

Life
as
Worship: PRAYER
AND PRAISE
IN JESUS' NAME

Introduction

A number of books about prayer are being published these days. And perhaps even more books currently available purport to help us pray or to provide aids to meditation. Why, then, have I written a book about prayer? Quite simply, because much of what is said on the subject seems to be so directly contrary to the character of Christian prayer, something true of both "conservative" and "liberal" interpretations of it. In an eager desire to commend prayer, certain people have said some extraordinary and extraordinarily unconvincing and superstitious things about it. Some say prayer will help us get what we want (it can even make our plants grow); others commend prayer as cheap therapy or a means to good mental health. In response to the old questions about unanswered prayer, they tell us to try harder, or, still worse, provide a series of outlandish excuses for God's deafness. The problem is that most of these books have gone wrong at the very start, because they focus upon the prayer life of individuals.

A. PRIVATE AND PUBLIC PRAYER

Talking a great deal about individual prayer is a very questionable practice. After all, are we not told that this is a private matter? The devotional guides and books exhorting people to more frequent, fervent prayer seem very much out of place, given Jesus' admonition to conduct one's praying in secret (Matt. 6:6).* Would not a certain amount of reticence be more

---

*When I am not translating passages, I am using the RSV. (Sometimes I cite the Lord's Prayer in its more familiar liturgical form, found in the ASV.)

appropriate than all the current promiscuous talk about how
to pray and the power of prayer?

Why, then, have I written a book about prayer? First of all,
this is not a book about private prayer; it is a book about public
prayer, the praying we do together, out loud. Despite what
Jesus said about prayer being private, we all do pray in public.
For example, we sometimes pray "out loud" with our families,
perhaps for and with a friend in distress. And all Christians
pray publicly in worship, if only to recite in unison the Lord's
Prayer. Others, especially clergy, must frequently pray in public, and are responsible for the pastoral prayer or for the selection of the common prayers of the congregation. This book
is about that sort of praying.

But this presents a problem: If praying is supposed to be
secret, why do we pray in public at all? Wouldn't it be better
to avoid public prayer altogether—especially if we are serious
about the authority of Jesus? This is a real problem, though
it is strange how seldom it occurs to us to think of it as one.[1]
But perhaps we can resolve the issue the same way we got
into it: by listening to what Jesus says about prayer.

When the disciples ask Jesus about prayer, he answers by
giving them a prayer. He explains nothing, but he does say,
"When you pray, say. . . ." This is very different advice from
that which is given by the current flood of books on the subject. Suppose you are a minister, and one of your parishioners
comes to you and says, "I just can't pray anymore. I don't
know how to do it, and it doesn't make any sense. . . ." The
spontaneous thing to do is to explain prayer or to encourage
him or her to pray more earnestly, more often, more regularly.
But Jesus says none of these things. He simply says, "When
you pray, say. . . ." He mentions nothing about mood, the right
frame of mind, the importance of prayer. I'm belaboring this
point a bit because we have forgotten to be startled by it. As

---

[1]The dilemma posed by the opposition between public prayer and Jesus'
admonition to pray in secret is seldom even recognized in the theological
discussion of prayer. Augustine recognized the problem and proposed a
resolution that has become standard: "It is not the being seen of men that
is wrong, but doing these things for the purpose of being seen of men" (*Our
Lord's Sermon on the Mount* [hereafter cited as *Sermon on the Mount*], III,
10 in *Nicene and Post-Nicene Fathers* [ed. P. Schaff, rpt. Eerdmans, 1956;
hereafter cited as *NPF*], VI [p. 37]).

is the case with most of what Jesus says, if we're not startled by it, we've missed the point altogether.

Jesus teaches his disciples to pray by giving them a prayer to say—it's as simple as that. Notice that Jesus doesn't display his own prayer life; he doesn't invite the disciples to listen to his private prayers. On the contrary, he keeps all of that completely hidden, secluding himself when he prays. The disciples are not to imitate his praying, but to say, "Our Father, who art in heaven. . . ." On the other hand, Ebeling has a point when he says that Jesus doesn't teach his disciples a prayer but shows them how to pray.[2] The point is that the Lord's Prayer isn't just another prayer, not even a new prayer (for one thing, we have two very different versions of it). It is a model for all prayer, a model that summarizes and epitomizes what prayer should be.[3]

In a similar way, praying in public serves the purpose of teaching people how to pray. *The public prayer of the congregation is the model for all prayer.* Congregational prayer is not therefore a promiscuous display of the essentially secret action of prayer; it is instead the formation of prayer, the summarizing of prayer.[4] We may say that it is the dramatic "acting-out" of prayer.

There are now two reasons for concentrating upon public prayer. The first is that it does not seem appropriate (not even permissible, perhaps) to discuss private prayer. The second is

---

[2]"Jesus did not seek to teach us a prayer, but to teach us to pray" (Gerhard Ebeling, *On Prayer*, Eng. tr. [Fortress, 1966], p. 47).

[3]In his treatise *On the Lord's Prayer* (*The Ante-Nicene Fathers* [ed. A. Roberts and J. Donaldson, rpt. Eerdmans, 1973; hereafter cited as *ANF*], V [pp. 447-457]), Cyprian refers to this prayer as "a form of praying" (2 [p. 448]). According to Augustine, the words of the Lord's Prayer represent the crucial ideas that govern prayer, so that by remembering the words we may "recollect those ideas at the time we pray" (*Sermon on the Mount*, III, 13 [p. 38]). In the same connection Johannes Wollebius may call this prayer "the form or true and religious pattern of prayer" (*Compendium Theologica Christianae* [1626], II, v, 2 in *Reformed Dogmatics*, ed. John W. Beardslee [Oxford, 1965], p. 204).

[4]So important is public prayer for the modeling of prayer generally that Calvin wrote, "We must consider that whoever refused to pray in the holy assembly of the godly knows not what it is to pray individually, or in a secret spot, or at home" (*Institutes of the Christian Religion* [ed. John T. McNeil, trans. Ford Lewis Battles, in the *Library of Christian Classics*, XXI (Westminster Press, 1960); hereafter cited as *Institutes*], III, xx, 29 [p. 892]).

that public prayer, the prayer which shapes all prayer, may be and *must* be publicly discussed. For if our public prayer is badly formed, it will adversely affect our understanding, practice, and experience of all prayer. Today many people—many of them Christians in the Church—find prayer difficult, meaningless, or unimportant. A surprising number of clergy report similar sentiments about prayer. Could this be due, at least in part, to the kind of prayer that people hear and say in public worship?

Some years ago, during the "death of God" controversy, someone "refuted" this theology by asserting, "I know God is alive. I spoke to him this morning." Although I think that this statement reveals a major misunderstanding of the death-of-God theology, it does suggest something important about prayer. It suggests that prayer isn't an isolated activity, but an activity related to the way we experience and think about God, and thus related to our perceptions of all manner of things— like hope and love—connected with faith. This means that badly formed, misinformed public prayer has an impact not only on the way people experience and practice prayer, but also on how people experience and think about everything related to their faith.

The public practice of prayer, then, is the only kind of prayer we *may* talk about. But it is urgent that we *do talk* about it, because it shapes all of our prayers, as well as our experience and understanding of faith as a whole.

B. PRAYER AND LIFESTYLE

We often think of worship as something quite separate from living, a separation that expresses itself in a number of ways. For instance, we put on our "Sunday best" in order to go to church. We worship in a specially constructed building in which often little or nothing else ever happens. We use different language "in church" than we use "in the world," and all too often the worship is conducted in a tone and manner which would be quite out of place elsewhere. The sermon, for example, is delivered in a "stained-glass voice," and the prayers are unnaturally elaborate and unctuous.

All of this points to a gulf between the religious and the

secular, between the holy and the profane. (*Profane* means "outside" or "before the temple," and thus distinct from what happens inside the temple.) This separation affects our understanding of prayer and praise, which we often think of as special actions and pious words quite separate from our everyday activity.

Now I believe that this understanding is a complete *mis*-understanding. Whatever may be true for worship in general, Christian worship is not dependent upon this distinction between the religious and the secular. Indeed, if our worship is genuine—i.e., done "in Jesus' name"—it overcomes this distinction and separation. I know that this will seem a rather startling position, but it is one which is derived quite straightforwardly from the central narratives and teachings of the New Testament. Rather than developing this theme exhaustively, I will only point to some of its most striking manifestations.

We may begin by attending to Mark's description of the death of Jesus—the event which is central to Mark's gospel and to Christian faith generally. Jesus' death is signaled by the rending of the veil of the Temple (Mark 15:38), which separates the holy space from the profane world. This event bears witness to the meaning of the crucifixion, and is reflected in John's apocalyptic vision. The New Jerusalem is expressly described as having "no temple" (Rev. 21:22). This must seem strange to those of us who like to think of the end of all things as the triumph of the Church, and the life beyond as an eternal church meeting. But it is quite clear from these passages that the goal of God's action is the end of religion.[5]

It is within this framework that it is possible to see the connection between a number of otherwise isolated texts. Take,

[5]On the overcoming of the distinction between the sacred and the profane as the meaning of the Christ-event, cf. Jürgen Moltmann, *The Church in the Power of the Spirit*, Eng. tr. (Harper & Row, 1977), pp. 267ff.; and Hans Küng, *The Church*, Eng. tr. (Sheed & Ward, 1967), pp. 363ff. No theologian in our time has seen this as clearly or argued it as forcefully as Thomas J. J. Altizer. While the much misunderstood phrase "the death of God" has a great complexity and richness in his thought, it does at least signify that God has acted to overcome the pseudo-reality of religion (and thus the reality of religion's god), and that this divine assault upon the religious barricade occurs in Jesus and continues with unremitting force even against and outside the church (Blake, Nietzsche, etc.). See *The Gospel of Christian Atheism* (Westminster, 1966).

for example, the story in Acts about Peter's vision, in which his religious scruples are overcome (Acts 10:9-34). The proclamation of the gospel to the (unclean) gentiles is equated with the eating of forbidden (unclean) food. The perennial effect of religion (not only Judaism) is this segregation of the clean from the unclean, the pure from the impure, the holy from the unholy, the godly from the godless—a discrimination which Peter's vision calls into question. In this vision Peter is confronted with the inner meaning of his Lord's teaching: "Man is not made for the Sabbath but the Sabbath for man" (Mark 2:27). In fact, Jesus' entire ministry can be seen as a prolonged assault upon the distinction between the clean and the unclean, the holy and the unholy. Is he not a friend of publicans and sinners? Is he not "a winebibber and a glutton"? (Luke 7:34).

Paul, whose basic point of view may be described by the phrase "the justification of the ungodly" (and therefore the overcoming of the distinction between the righteous and the unrighteous), applies this principle to worship itself. He condemns the setting aside of "days" and "seasons" as a regression into pre-Christian superstition (Gal. 4:10). When someone raises the question about eating meat consecrated to other gods, he undercuts the whole basis for the dispute: "Whether you eat or abstain from eating, do all to the glory of God" (I Cor. 10:31; Rom. 14:6).

But what, then, is permissible when we worship God? Only this: that we present to God our bodies (Rom. 12:1)—that is, our life in the world in all its relationships and connections.[6] Worship is not primarily a matter of special practices but a matter of lifestyle.

This critique of religion is not the "discovery" of Christianity. The prophets of Israel had already thundered Yahweh's condemnation of feasts, sacrifices, and other "religious practices" (Amos 5:21-24), and the historians of Israel had already depicted Yahweh's extreme reluctance to permit the building of a temple (II Sam. 7:1-29). We know of the prohibitions of graven images, which are the very heart of the attempt to rep-

---

[6]This notion of "body" is suggested by Ernst Käsemann in "Primitive Christian Apocalyptic," *New Testament Questions of Today*, Eng. tr. (Fortress, 1969), p. 135.

resent God's holiness with a "holy object" (Exodus 20:4). All of this is intensified and focused in the New Testament.

We are not speaking here of the displacement of our old (and false) religion by a new (and true) religion. Both Judaism and Christianity know that God is at war with religion, and both have sided against God by turning themselves into religions. Bear in mind that I am using the word "religion" in a special sense: to identify the tendency to separate certain times, places, attitudes, actions, objects, and words from all others. These things "set apart" are made the special province of faith, the special marks of piety, separated from contamination by the world, by the unrighteous. This results in "religious temptation," which takes many forms. In our own time it may take the form of an individualistic piety or a metaphysical supernaturalism—that, at least, is the way Bonhoeffer diagnoses our modern religious temptation.[7] We put faith into the airtight containers of individual piety or put God into the airtight container of "transcendence" or "the supernatural." This separation means that God and faith are sealed off from "real life," from our daily existence. When Bonhoeffer called for "a non-religious interpretation" of the central images and actions of faith, he was calling for an overcoming of this separation and compartmentalization.

This separation and compartmentalization takes other forms as well. We may notice it in the way in which the Church customarily isolates itself from political and economic issues. This isolation results in the Church's siding with the political and economic status quo, and therefore against the poor and the captive. We may detect it in the preoccupation with special experiences and a special language characteristic of some forms of the charismatic revival. The result may be the intrusion of pious phrases into all conversation, or even the ostentatious display of glossalalia. We may also see it in the requirements of fundamentalism, which produces a split-level consciousness—believing one thing on Sunday and something else the rest of the week.

Above all we may notice the forms this compartmentali-

[7]Bonhoeffer identifies religion with "metaphysics" and "inwardness" in *Letters and Papers from Prison* (6/4/44; 7/8/44), ed. E. Bethge, Eng. tr. (Macmillan, 1953), pp. 195-198 and pp. 213f.

zation takes in "mainline" churches. It is characteristic of our church life that we encourage people to be preoccupied with the church—its institutional preservation, the development of its program. Ministers and lay people get on a treadmill of church busyness. We even have a hierarchy of participants: at the bottom are those who attend church on Christmas and Easter, followed by those who "are regular in attendance," those who perform some responsible function in the program of the church, those who are there every time the doors are open, those who devote themselves to "fulltime Christian service" (ministers and the like), and, finally, those who put in eighty or more hours a week ("good" ministers). This hierarchy is insidious, destructive, and idolatrous for a number of reasons. But for our purposes here it is enough to say that it feeds upon and promotes the "religious temptation." Church life in America (and perhaps that in other countries) is characterized by a complete preoccupation with religion and a corresponding neglect of the Gospel.

Bonhoeffer's call for a nonreligious interpretation of faith is therefore an urgent one for us. To engage in a "nonreligious interpretation" does not mean to get rid of words like "God," "Christ," "Spirit," and "prayer." This may be the goal of "secularization," but it is not the goal of theology.[8] That goal must be to show how these things alter and interpret our lives as men and women in the world. We are not to choose between the false claims of "religion" and "secularity," but to overcome this separation because of God's action in Christ.

We must therefore attempt a "non-religious" interpretation of prayer. This will not mean that we concentrate on prayer as "meditation"[9] or "self-therapy" or "auto-suggestion." All of these things may be important for what Barth called a

---

[8]Bonhoeffer explicitly renounces a "reductionism" as the meaning of a non-religious interpretation in *Letters and Papers from Prison* (6/8/44), pp. 199f. This distinction between a liberal (or existential or "secular") reductionism and a true non-religious interpretation is one that is regularly overlooked by many who appropriate Bonhoeffer's idea without troubling to discern its content or context.

[9]The rich tradition of contemplative and meditational exercises in the Christian community has a value and importance of its own; I only wish to make as clear as possible the distinction between these exercises and prayer.

"psychic hygiene," much like doing push-ups or brushing one's teeth are important for physical hygiene. But these things have nothing whatever to do with prayer. Prayer is speaking to God, and if a prayer is not addressed to God, it is not prayer. I no more oppose meditation than I oppose jogging, but neither of them should be confused with prayer.

To engage in a non-religious interpretation of prayer will mean that we must understand prayer from the standpoint of the mission and ministry, the life and destiny of Jesus of Nazareth. This will be the vantage point that determines everything else. The key to everything is praying "in Jesus' name" or "for Jesus' sake," which is the sign and seal of authentic Christian prayer. Exploring what it means to pray "in Jesus' name" will enable us to cut away a veritable jungle of superstitious misconceptions about prayer. It will also enable us to clearly distinguish appropriate kinds of prayer from those which are blasphemous, idolatrous, and superstitious.

This concern with prayer "in Jesus' name" is not a concern for a mere formula. Indeed, whether or not this formula is present in our prayers is a matter of little importance; even the Lord's Prayer does not contain it. Furthermore, the mere presence of the formula does not in any way assure us that the prayer is truly a Christian prayer. Our concern is whether our public prayers are compatible with Christ's mission and ministry, whether our prayers are in keeping with what God has done and promised in and through Jesus. It may very well be the case that many of the prayers of Jews and Moslems are compatible with God's act and promise in Jesus, whereas some of the prayers of the Christian community are not. As a Christian theologian I do not have the task of evaluating the public prayers of Jews or Moslems. But I may and must ask of the public prayers of Christian communities: to what extent do these prayers conform to the standard which they themselves proclaim—that they are spoken in the name and for the sake of Jesus.

But if prayer "in Jesus' name" is not primarily a religious act with a separate religious meaning, what, then, is its meaning? To give a non-religious interpretation of prayer "in Jesus' name" is to ask, how does this prayer shape our everyday life in the world? Only if prayer (and praise) affects our daily existence can it truly be prayer "in the name of Jesus." Only thus will it testify to the overcoming of the separation between the holy and the unholy, the sacred and the profane, God and the world.

Our public worship has a form and order called "liturgy," which means the work or action (*erga*) of the people. As God's people, our work is not only—or even primarily—"spiritual" or "churchly" activity; it is principally the way we live in the world. Thus Paul encourages the Christians under his care to present their "bodies as a reasonable worship" (Rom. 12:1)— that is, to worship through all their relationships and activities. Our life is our proper worship: it is a "reasonable" (rational, intentional, ordered) worship to the extent to which it has discernable shape or form. The task of liturgy, in the narrow sense, is to provide this order. Thus what we do together in our Sunday worship orders and models our true worship: liturgy shapes lifestyle.[10] That liturgy shapes lifestyle means, of course, that it is not an act of separation, but an act that overcomes religion, that reconciles the world to God.

Now we can see how important the prayers of our public worship are: they not only shape all our other prayers and our perception of God and his actions, but they provide the model for our everyday life in the world. If the prayers which we say in public are formless or falsely formed, then our lives may be similarly malformed. On the other hand, paying attention to the language and the proper character of our prayer will enable us to live in ways which are more clearly in keeping with our identity as Christians.

This makes it imperative that in our consideration of prayer and praise we give particular attention to the lifestyle summarized and formed by prayer "in Jesus' name." In the chapters entitled "Prayer as Formation" and "Praise as Formation," we will discuss the ways in which our life is formed by the words of public and corporate speech directed toward God.

C. PRAYER AND PRAISE

In order to understand prayer, we must distinguish between

[10]Cf. the excellent article by Don Saliers, "Prayer and Lifestyle," in *Christians at Prayer*, ed. John Gallen, S.J. (Notre Dame, 1977), pp. 46-60.

prayer and praise. Both are "odd" in the sense that they are ways of speaking not about but *to* God. On the basis of this similarity they are often spoken of together, so we may speak of a "prayer of thanksgiving" even though thanksgiving is praising God. Up to this point we have followed this common usage, but from now on we will sharply distinguish prayer from praise.

The difference between prayer and praise is both deceptively simple and deeply significant. On the one hand it is like the difference between "please" and "thank you." We say "please" when we want what we don't have; we say "thank you" when we have gotten what we want. But this simple difference is also profound. In prayer we express the absence of something; in praise, the presence of something. In both cases that "something" is the same thing—God. The difference between prayer and praise, then, is the difference between the absence and the presence of God. It is difficult to imagine a more profound difference, yet it is frequently ignored. Sometimes people even speak of God's presence in connection with prayer. This makes for total confusion (unless, of course, we mean prayer to include praise and thanksgiving—that is, all speaking to God).

By sharply distinguishing between prayer and praise, we will be able to understand the true character of each. The distinction will at first produce some rather jarring and apparently strange results, but these results will also help to "solve" some otherwise murky problems. Only on the basis of this distinction can we satisfactorily clarify our understanding of the problem of "unanswered prayer," or the reason for praying even though God presumably already knows what we need. This distinction can also free both our prayer and our praise to become more honest and more truthful. Our prayer is freed to become more bold, and our praise, more joyful. In this way both become less contrived and artificial, more "natural" and spontaneous.

Though prayer and praise stand in stark contrast to one another, they nevertheless belong together. Both are addressed to God, both are spoken "in the name and for the sake of Jesus," both shape our lives. Thus the discussion of one clarifies the other. Our worship and our lives are structured or

formed by the alternation between prayer and praise, and de-
fining this alternation will clarify the relationship between
them. The goal of distinguishing between prayer and praise
is to make clear their ultimate unity, which will be the subject
of the last chapter of this book.

In the following chapters we will explore the character of
prayer and praise "in Jesus' name." This will mean first asking about the basic character of prayer and praise. What are the
basic features, the invariable characteristics of prayers which
are not only verbally but also essentially spoken in the name
of Jesus? What are the unvarying characteristics of praise which
make it both like and unlike prayer? Because we are concerned
with prayer and praise in the public worship of the community, we will have to examine the major types of prayer and
praise. In the discussion of prayer this will mean examining
invocation, petition, and intercession; in discussing praise we
will look at adoration (the Gloria Patri, the doxology, etc.),
thanksgiving, rejoicing, and offering. We will also have to ask
how both prayer and praise shape the kind of life which is
"prayer without ceasing" or "continuous praise." This three-
fold division corresponds to three basic features of our interpretation of prayer: 1) that it is offered in the name of Jesus;
2) that we must concern ourselves with public prayer (not
speaking directly about what is essentially secret); 3) that the
elements of our public worship must not be merely "religious," separated from the world, but must provide the model
for our everyday life.

In order to avoid some of the most common misunderstandings of our speaking to God in the name of Jesus, we will
deal first with prayer and then with praise. The final chapter
will reunite these two elements of our life and worship.

PART I:
Prayer in Jesus' Name

My prayers must meet a brazen heaven
and fail or scatter all away.
Unclean and seeming unforgiven
My prayers I scarcely call to pray.
I cannot buoy my heart above;
Above it cannot entrance win.
I reckon precedents of love,
But feel the long success of sin.

My heaven is brass and iron my earth:
Yea iron is mingled with my clay
So harden'd is it in this dearth
Which prayng fails to do away.
Nor tears, nor tears this clay uncouth
Could mould, if any tears there were.
A warfare of my lips in truth,
Battling with God, is now my prayer.

Gerard Manley Hopkins,
"My prayers must meet a brazen heaven"

ATTEMPTING to speak clearly and critically about prayer is difficult. By concentrating upon the role of prayer in our public worship, we can avoid many of the dangers inherent in a promiscuous display of personal piety. But beyond this we must recognize the often unnoticed difficulty involved in the movement from "talking to" God to "talking about" prayer. Prayer is an address to God that is not concerned with any other "audience." But in talking *about* prayer we are the audience, and we must stand back and examine the way we speak to God in public.

In discussing prayer we must also be critical—we must ask whether a particular sort of prayer is appropriate, whether it properly conforms to the true character of prayer. If the practice of prayer has become distorted, as I believe it has, this will mean making negative judgments about many prayers. Such critical investigation is necessary, because it is in this way that theology attempts to assist the community in becoming more faithful and attaining maturity. But this critical approach is very different from the spontaneous prayer that is a "sighing too deep for words." It must therefore be remembered that here we are scrutinizing corporate and public prayers, not secret prayer. Secret prayer is the heart's free and spontaneous address to God which must not be hemmed in by theological judgments. For this reason Barth is quite right in saying that secret prayer "is from the very outset free from all care. It does not have to be beautiful or edifying, logically coherent or theologically correct."[1] But when prayer is public and corporate we must subject it to theological—and therefore critical—scrutiny, because, as we have seen, this form of prayer may help or hinder all praying, all belief, all life.

[1] Karl Barth, *Church Dogmatics*, Eng. tr. (T. & T. Clark, 1936-1962), III/4, p. 88.

CHAPTER ONE
The Shape of Prayer

The prayers of Christians, no matter how diverse, all share certain elements. These constant features of prayer "in all times and in all places" constitute the unity of the one prayer of God's people. But in seeking to discover this underlying structure of prayer, we will continually have to ask ourselves what prayer is truly prayer "in Jesus' name." This means that we will have to be particularly careful lest our prayers become only nominally rather than actually joined with the prayer of Jesus. To this end it will be especially necessary to use as our touchstone the prayer which Jesus taught his disciples.[1] This will help us to gain a better grasp of the essentials of prayer and to expose those travesties that masquerade as Christian prayer but that are in reality superstitious and idolatrous substitutes for it.

Although the degeneration of prayer in our churches compels me to be more polemical than I would like to be in distinguishing Christian prayer from idolatrous prayer, it is not my aim to chastise the church and its leaders but to make it possible for us all to pray more boldly, more truthfully, and more confidently. To do so we must clear away some of the misconceptions about prayer which have gained currency in some of our churches and which have weakened or destroyed the prayer of our congregations. Many (though by no means all) of the dilemmas regarding prayer arise from the misun-

---

[1]Tertullian rightly termed this prayer "an epitome of the whole Gospel" (*On Prayer, ANF*, III, i [p. 681]). Most of the theological treatises on prayer, from the time of Tertullian (whose treatise is the first in this line) to the present, have taken the form of a commentary on this prayer in its Matthean form (excluding the doxology). The procedure adopted here is not that of a verse-by-verse commentary but of regular attention to the prayer as a whole.

derstanding and the malpractice of prayer. These shortcomings may be corrected only as we more clearly discern the essential features of that prayer which is truly offered "in Jesus' name."

A. AN ADDRESS TO GOD

The most obvious thing about prayer is this: it is an address to God. This is the form which prayer takes whenever we encounter it "in public." Some may argue that there is a higher form of prayer which disper es with words, a private form of prayer which is union with God. That may be true, but such communion does not provide the model of all prayer, nor does it provide the context in which prayer is overheard. When you or I pray, if we do, we say something to God.

Frankly, this may be the most astonishing feature of prayer: that it is talking to God. People engage in other activities that are sometimes called praying—silent meditation, mystical contemplation, quiet reflection. In comparison to these things, ordinary prayer may seem crude and naive, but so be it. Our aim is to understand ordinary prayer, the kind anyone can hear, or overhear, any Sunday morning in any church.

I said that it was obvious that praying is talking to God. In fact, it is so obvious that it is regularly forgotten, especially by people who pray frequently in public. The formal, established, or liturgical prayers which are prayed in any church are obviously addressed to God. But the extemporaneous or pastoral prayers, usually said by the minister or priest, often only *seem* to be addressed to God; more often they are addressed to the congregation. The form is correct, and they begin as if they were addressed to God: "Our Father," "Almighty God," "Dear Lord." The trouble begins almost immediately thereafter. This becomes obvious when we ask, what is this prayer being used to do? Certain prayers are used to make announcements, impressing upon their listeners the importance of attending the next worship service, the meeting of the Board of Trustees, the potluck being sponsored by the women's group, or the youth group's car wash. Other prayers are used to reinforce the sermon—to drive home the point, to claim divine sanction for the preacher's opinion, to decorate the homily or to repeat it. Just count the number of times the following phrases come up: "Help us to remember . . . ," "Help us to know . . . ," "Make us mindful of . . . ," "Impress upon us. . . ."

Such prayers illustrate one very powerful reason why people find prayer meaningless, difficult, and empty. It has nothing to do with lack of faith, with secularity, with the well-known ravages of modernity. It is the direct result of prayers that are addressed to ourselves. People don't learn to be practical atheists by getting too involved in the world; they learn it in church—in the prayers they hear in church. If we address ourselves and one another in our prayers, it is small wonder that they don't seem to go anywhere, that the sky like a leaden vault only echoes our empty words. All the books and sermons on prayer cannot prevail against the factual evidence that such prayer is a meaningless exercise in auto-suggestion. This evidence is not presented by skeptics outside the church; it is paraded about and underscored in the prayers that we well-intentioned people regularly offer in church and at home. We are our own worst enemies when it comes to prayer. Until we learn this hard and bitter lesson, and we drastically change the character of the prayers we pray in public, our churches will remain the single biggest obstacle to the life of true prayer.

In short, if we use prayer to speak to ourselves or to one another, we destroy it.[2] That is the first consequence of the

---

[2]Barth's formulation is admirable: "Prayer as a demonstration of faith, as disguised preaching, as an instrument of edification, is obviously not prayer at all. Prayer is not prayer if it is addressed to anyone else but God" (*Church Dogmatics*, III/4, p. 88). Yet this is by no means the "common wisdom" of the theological tradition. This principle is regularly subverted by the question, Since God already knows what we need, why should we ask at all? It was all too easy to respond to this question with the edifying reflection that we are really addressing ourselves. This catastrophic notion is erected into a principle by Augustine, who repeatedly asserts that, in prayer, "we admonish ourselves" (*Letter CXXX* ["To Proba"], ii, 21 in *NPF*, I, pp. 465ff.). Aquinas is only taking over this position when he writes, "We need to pray to God not in order to make known to him our needs and desires but that we ourselves may be reminded of having recourse to God's help in these matters" (*Summa Theologica*, II, II, Q. 83, Art. 2, p. 1539. Note: I am using the translation published by Benziger Brothers, New York, 1947, which is "literally translated by Fathers of the English Dominican Province."). Similarly, John Wesley concludes, "So that the end of Prayer is not to inform God, as though he knew not your wants already, but rather to inform ourselves" (*Sermon XXI, Wesley's Standard Sermons*, ed. Sugden [Epworth, 1955], p. 431).

recognition that prayer is speaking to God. In prayer we dare
not be preoccupied with ourselves—not our feelings, our desires, nor anything else. These may have their place in prayer,
but prayer is above all directed to and focused upon God.

But what do our public prayers communicate about God?
Who is this God who is addressed? Over the last couple of
centuries in the West we have supposed that our worst enemy
was atheism, and our greatest necessity to get people to believe
in God—any god. This is the meaning of the "great debate"
between atheism and theism. But in truth this debate is not
very important. Christianity's most virulent opponent has always been superstition rather than atheism; false gods are far
worse than no god at all. It was because they understood this
quite clearly that the early Christians were frequently accused
of being atheists themselves, something we have almost completely forgotten. As a result, our churches have become
seedbeds of every imaginable form of pagan superstition, a
development nowhere more evident than in the prayers we
offer "in Jesus' name."[3] Simply examine the prayers we pray
in public: write them down and study them. Apart from the
all too often merely routine "conclusion"—"in Jesus' name"—
to whom are they really addressed? To which God are we
praying:

> to some private tooth fairy or to the Lord of creation?
> to some passive deity or to the God who acts?
> to some distant and alien being or to our Father?
> to some anonymous supreme being or to the Father of
>   Jesus?
> to the grantor of our wishes or to the Savior of the world?

It is, unfortunately, only a short step from "reminding ourselves" to
reminding others, and thus to the "homiletical" prayer that destroys all
prayer. Barth and subsequently Jacques Ellul in *Prayer and Modern Man*,
Eng. tr. (Seabury, 1970), prevent this dissolution by recourse to the "command of God," which needs no justification or explanation. Unfortunately,
it is difficult to justify the assertion that prayer is "the command of God,"
because it nowhere becomes the subject of a special and direct exhortation
in the Old or New Testament, but is more often "presupposed." Only through
a consideration of God's absence and his promise (which I undertake in the
following pages) does it seem to me possible to make clear how our prayer
may and must be directed to God.

[3]Cf. Shirley C. Guthrie, Jr., "The Narcissism of American Piety: The
Disease and the Cure," *Journal of Pastoral Care*, 31, Dec. 1977, 220-229.
I agree with Guthrie's diagnosis of the disease, though I don't agree alto-
gether with the "cure."

to the universal tinkerer or to the One who raises the dead?
to the candy machine in the sky or to the Judge of heaven
and earth?
to the great magician or to the One who for our sakes became poor, weak, mortal, even died upon the cross?

Do our prayers spring from and form faith, or do they spring
from and cultivate unbelief or superstition?

By drawing attention to what is most obvious about prayer,
we already begin to understand some of our problems with
prayer. One theme that we will return to many times is this:
our public prayers *seem* empty and meaningless because they
are, because they overlook, forget, or falsify the most basic
and obvious characteristic of prayer—that it is speaking to
God.

B. THE CALL FOR GOD

Our prayers to God primarily take the form of a request, a
petition. Indeed, this is the meaning of the word "prayer"
itself. Outside its specifically religious use, it means, simply,
a plea. But what does it mean to beseech God? For what, after
all, do we ask? To answer this question we must turn to the
basic prayers of the Christian community: the Lord's Prayer
and the "maranatha" of the earliest Christian communities.

The Lord's Prayer is that prayer which, according to Matthew (6:9-13) and Luke (1:2-4), Jesus taught his disciples to
pray.[4] For that reason it is the basic prayer of the gathered
Christian community, serving as the true test and the instruc-
tive model of all Christian prayer within that community.[5]
The fundamental petition of the Lord's Prayer and thus of all
Christian prayer is the plea for God's coming, for God's rule and

[4] Throughout we will note both the differences and the similarities of
these versions of the prayer. It is usual to comment only on the Matthean
version of the prayer, although Origen devoted considerable attention to the
differences. The only identical constructions in the two versions are the
first two petitions: "hallowed be your name" and "your kingdom come." In
general the Matthean version is greatly expanded. For a contemporary commentary, cf. Ernst Lohmeyer, *"Our Father": An Introduction to the Lord's
Prayer*, Eng. tr. (Harper & Row, 1966); Joachim Jeremias, *The Prayers of
Jesus* (Fortress, 1978); Philip B. Harner, *The Lord's Prayer* (Fortress, 1975).

[5] "... if we pray rightly and as becomes our wants, we say nothing but
what is already contained in the Lord's prayer" (Augustine, *Letter CXXX*,
xii, 22 [p. 466]).

God's kingdom. This is the meaning of the three-fold petition that opens and thus dominates the Lord's Prayer: "hallowed be your name, your kingdom come, your will be done on earth as it is in heaven." Let us examine each of these petitions individually.

The first petition, "hallowed be your name," may also be translated as "make your name holy" or "sanctify your name." This petition may sound strange to our ears. What might it mean for God's name to be sanctified? Surely God is holy! This request is all the more puzzling when we recall that the name of God is, in this context, not something separate from God himself: it is God in his power, in his manifestation of himself.[6] The petition is therefore tantamount to asking God to make himself holy or—and now we come to the heart of the matter—that God be God. The initial petition then places upon God the demand that he be "true to himself," that he become who he is. This is an extraordinary petition, an astonishing request, one that we will return to repeatedly in the course of our reflections upon prayer. It is far from being an outmoded and merely quaint form of prayer: it is the heart and core of *every* prayer. When all is said and done, this is the only prayer offered by the Christian community: hallowed be your name, sanctify your name, make your name holy, be true to yourself, be God.[7]

[6]This is now the general view of biblical scholarship, but it is by no means a recent discovery. Origen knew this already (*On Prayer* in *Alexandrian Christianity*, ed. H. Chadwick, in the *Library of Christian Classics*, II [Westminster, 1954], XXIV, 2-3 [p. 288]); and Wesley's formulation is quite exact: "The name of God is God Himself; the nature of God, so far as it can be discovered to man" (*Sermon XXI, Wesley's Standard Sermons*, p. 435).

[7]With the loss of an eschatological perspective, this petition became quite difficult to understand. Luther psychologizes it (in *Small Catechism*) to mean that we pray here for the proper attitude of respect toward God, thereby echoing the position of Augustine (*Sermon on the Mount*, V, 19 [p. 40]). Calvin's view is somewhat more "objective" because he maintains that "we are bidden to request not only that God vindicate his sacred name of all contempt and dishonor but also that he subdue the whole race of mankind to reverence for it" (*Institutes*, III, xx, 41 [p. 904]). Yet even this does not seem to go far enough. The point of the petition is that in "vindicating his name" (and only in so doing) does God truly become God. Gerhard Ebeling's formulation is therefore to be preferred: " 'Hallowed be thy name' is as much as to say: Holy One become holy, God become God— in time, in the reality of this world, in history" (*On Prayer*, p. 56).

The second of these petitions, "your kingdom come," seems quite different. In it the petitioner directs his attention toward that absolute future which is God's reign. That which we need and desire comes to us from that future,[8] but what is it? It is indeed nothing other than God's rule, a rule which is his presence, finally and fully manifest.

A variety of images are used for this anticipated reign of God. Both the accounts of Jesus' exorcisms and healings as well as the closing depiction in the Apocalypse of John ("there will be no more death, and no more mourning or sadness") point to God's reign as the time of healing and health (Rev. 21:4; cf. Isa. 25:8). Other images pick up the socio-political implications of the term "kingdom," depicting God's rule as a time of justice and peace among the nations. Perhaps the most prominent images are those of the messianic and wedding banquets used by Jesus himself. They suggest eating and drinking and companionship, which dispel forever the spectre of want and need and isolation. Still others point to the new creation which results in a new heaven and a new earth (II Peter 3:13; cf. Isa. 65:17), concomitant (according to Paul) with the restoration to life of those who have fallen under the power of God's last enemy—death itself (I Cor. 15:26). Most comprehensively, God's reign is the abolition of every barrier between God and his creation, making God "everything to everyone" (I Cor. 15:28). As the Apocalypse of John expresses it, there will be neither temple nor sun nor moon in the new Jerusalem because God himself, and the Lamb, shall dwell there (Rev. 21:22). These images—and we have merely suggested the wealth of images found in the New Testament— have a threefold importance.

First, by their multiplicity and extravagance they make clear that no existing or attainable state of affairs within history can be confused with what God promises to his people and his creation. This means that Christian existence is always looking toward a future which vastly exceeds every present, and

[8]Ebeling: "Prayer is turning toward the future" (*On Prayer*, p. 61). Unfortunately, it seems to me that Ebeling proceeds to render this future almost entirely in present and private terms in the remainder of his sermon on "Thy kingdom come." This "existential" perspective is not the only one for him, however, as is shown in his reflection on the "third petition."

to that degree is always in tension with every existing state of affairs. Indeed, insofar as any spiritual, political, economic, or psychological status quo seeks to absolutize itself, Christian existence opposes and contradicts it.

Despite the tension produced by anticipating an absolute future, that for which Christians hope is not an ethereal and, in the popular sense, unworldly future. Put most simply, the future for which Christians hope is not a "disembodied" one. On the contrary, the images characterizing God's kingdom point to the transformation of—not escape from—the earth, the body, and society. Thus, in the accounts of Jesus' ministry, the healing of men's and women's bodies and the transformation of ordinary water into intoxicating wine are the indicators of the approach of God's reign. Saint Paul never speaks of the "immortality of the soul"—only of the resurrection of the body. That for which we hope is therefore a transformation including all dimensions of earthly and bodily life.

Finally, these images make clear that what we hope for is nothing other than the drawing near of God himself. We are not dealing here with two separate things: it is precisely God's presence and nearness which constitutes this transformation of earthly life. We are not presented with a choice between "spiritual" values and corporal ones, between idealism and materialism, between heaven and earth. We are promised both a new heaven and a new earth (II Peter 3:13). In all of this there is a clear order. It is because God draws near that "the blind see, the lame walk, lepers are cleansed, and the deaf hear . . ." (Luke 7:22). This transformation of the flesh is not an independent event or an added benefit of God's coming. It is what happens when the Creator of earth and Parent of all flesh draws near and comes into his own.

This means, then, that the prayer for the coming of God's kingdom is a prayer for the coming of God himself. It is an appeal to God to be really and truly God, to be God for us and with us, to reign as Lord of creation. Like the petition "hallowed be thy name," this petition is the entreaty to God to be God—it is, simply, the cry for God.

To these two petitions found in both Luke and Matthew (and the only petitions found in exactly the same form in both accounts), Matthew adds a third parallel petition: "thy will be done." This might also be translated, "your goal come to fruition."[9] The reference here is clearly not to a series of un-related decisions or willings on God's part, but to this ultimate aim or goal, God's final intention. Nor are we left to guess about what this ultimate aim or goal may be—it is by no means inscrutable. To put it bluntly, it is "the salvation of the world." Nothing less than this can conform to that petition, for noth-ing less than this is the goal of the one whom Jesus calls "Father."

To the three petitions Matthew adds the further phrase "on earth as it is in heaven." This phrase qualifies all three peti-tions, not only the last.[10] It asks of God that he hallow his name on earth just as it is "in heaven," that he bring his rule to earth as he rules "in heaven," that his aim be accomplished on earth as it is "in heaven." This is an audacious prayer indeed, though it is implicit in the petitions which it sum-marizes and qualifies. In effect it says: It is not enough that you be holy in yourself—be holy to us as well; it is not enough that you reign far off, far above, far ahead—rule here and now; it is not enough that your goal is perfect in itself—complete it here. In short, it says: It is not enough that you are God— be God for us, with us here and now.

Abraham bargained with God to spare a town for the sake of a few righteous men. Jesus teaches his disciples to place a far greater claim upon God—that he save the world—for his

---

[9]Perhaps the best literal translation is this: "Finish your goal [let it have been brought into being]." There is no warrant in the text for the psychol-ogizing and moralizing interpretations that are typically affixed to this petition.

[10]Of the theologians of the pre-modern period, only Origen seems to have recognized that this phrase "to be found in Matthew alone, can be taken with all three clauses" (*On Prayer*, XXVI, 2 [p. 292]). Yet attention to the text makes this abundantly clear. The three petitions are formed in exact parallel to one another, a paralleling that cannot be translated but which might be represented as follows:

Sanctify your name
Bring your reign
Accomplish your goal

The parallel is completely abandoned by the phrase "as in heaven, so on earth" which "rhymes" with, and so refers to, the opening clause "who art in heaven." The opening clause and the concluding clause are both Matthew's additions (or at least found only in Matthew), and so must be considered together. They contain the three petitions within a field of ten-sion, the tension between "in heaven" and "on earth."

own sake. It is an astonishing prayer, and it is even more astonishing that we often repeat it as absent-mindedly as if we were asking the grocer for a box of crackers.

The "maranatha" (I Cor. 16:22) may be the earliest extant prayer of the Christian community—the oldest fragment of liturgy. It means "Lord, come," and is reiterated at the conclusion of the Apocalypse of John (Rev. 22:20). This is not an additional prayer alongside the Lord's Prayer. It is the most compact summary of that prayer and all its petitions. Indeed, it is the summary of all petitions which the community and its members may make, because it is in his coming that Jesus is made manifest to all as Lord, and it is only in his lordship that all that we pray for is answered and fulfilled. This prayer, then, is the petition that Jesus exercise his lordship not only privately but openly; not only in his resurrection but in ours as well; not only "in heaven" but also "on earth." It is thus an imperative: be who you are, be the Lord. In the fullest and most final sense, Jesus is not yet this, even though he may be this for the community which bears his name. For both Christians and Jews, the Lord is he who is to come. Both communities yearn for the same consummation; both have their existence in this yearning, this plea, this hope. The Christian community, however, claims to know the name of the one who will come, and in whose coming is comprised God's rule; thus it prays for the coming of God's reign "in Jesus' name" and prays "maranatha"—"Lord, come."

Our consideration of the Lord's Prayer and of the "maranatha" shows that these are not two prayers but one. It further shows that what we pray for is God: God's presence in his name, his kingdom, his goal, his Son. In all of this we simply pray that God will be God, that he be who he promises to be. As Christians we do not pray for many things but for one thing: for God's reign.[11] Only insofar as the many re-

[11]That the first three petitions of the Lord's Prayer amount to a single petition is implicitly maintained by Calvin (*Institutes*, III, xx, 43-44 [p. 907]), and explicitly by Wollebius (*Compendium Theologica Christianae* [p. 204]). Concerning all three petitions Barth writes: "He neither compromises Himself nor does He overload us. He wills and demands of us that which is proper to us in relation to him, and therefore just our asking, but primarily and basically our asking for the advance and triumph of His own cause" (*Church Dogmatics*, III/4, p. 104).

quests are included in this single request do we have any claim upon them or make any place for them. If a prayer cannot be summarized as the demand that God be God, it cannot be prayed "in Jesus' name."

C. THE ABSENCE OF GOD

On what basis can or do we speak to God? What particular attitude does the act of praying presuppose? All too often the answer given this question is that we need a sense of God's presence, of his availability and nearness—in short, that some religious or pious precondition must be met. If the greatest malpractice of prayer stems from directing prayer to someone or something other than God, then the greatest misunderstanding of prayer comes from the assumption that prayer has a "religious presupposition." If prayer has such a presupposition, then the prayer for God to be God is meaningless. If God is present to us in and through our piety, what is the point of asking for that presence? If God rules in ways that we find satisfactory, why should we pray for that rule? If we regard God's goal as already realized, what is the purpose of praying that this goal be accomplished? Two fairly typical stories may help us explore this matter more concretely.

Many of us have at times asked, "God seems so far away. How can I pray?" The question is an ache in the heart, a half-benumbed soreness that throbs when the religious "expert" commends prayer to us. How can any of the aids to prayer relieve this deep ache? The words of the experts may sometimes numb the ache—or succeed in making us ashamed of it and wish to hide it (much as we might tell the dentist that it doesn't hurt when we press *there*). But the ache remains. And the words of the prayers that we read in the books, that we hear on Sunday, that we try to "say" at rare occasions during the week are perhaps quite edifying—but empty.

When I was away at college, my uncle, who was a career Marine, would occasionally invite me to his home (located in the same state as my school). He knew I was studying to be a minister, and this embarrassed him, because he was not a particularly religious man. To cover his embarrassment he would regularly assure me, with a declaration that became a kind of litany, "There's no such thing as an atheist in a fox-hole." I found this reassurance somewhat embarrassing, because I rather vaguely felt that praying when other people were shooting at you wasn't exactly a model form of prayer. I'd heard a few sermons that had made it clear that religion used for emergencies was next to no religion at all. On the other hand, my uncle had been in quite a few foxholes, and the preachers of those sermons hadn't—and neither had I. I had the sense to keep my mouth shut.

To what condition of our lives do the prayers we offer correspond? Much—far too much—has been written about the "mood" or "atmosphere" for prayer. Much is made of "getting in the proper frame of mind" or "having the right attitude," and very often this attitude is somehow associated with a sense of God's presence. As a consequence, various aids are proposed for conjuring up this attitude. Far from helping people to pray, however, such an emphasis often has the opposite effect, providing a ready-made excuse not to pray. If God seems distant, and the skies made of resounding brass, prayer seems inappropriate or impossible.

All of this is, I believe, the result of a serious confusion and misunderstanding. *If prayer has any basis at all in what we feel about God, it has that basis not in our sense of God's presence but in our sense of God's absence.* No matter what else will have to be said about prayer, that is the beginning and the end. If we don't start there, then nothing that we say about prayer will make any sense, because *only in God's absence is it possible and meaningful to pray for God's presence.* The simple assertion that prayer corresponds to God's absence is the sharp edge that we must use to clear away the jungle of well-meant platitudes about prayer—platitudes that, in "defending" prayer, make it impossible for countless people.

There is, then, no religious presupposition, no spiritual prerequisite for prayer. Prayer's only basis is in our godless-ness and godforsakenness, the only precondition for meaning-ful, necessary prayer. If God is fully present with us, prayer is neither necessary nor possible (although, as we shall see, praise and thanksgiving become possible and necessary at those times).

I have stressed this point repeatedly because it is so often missed in expositions of prayer, perhaps because it is so obvious. A few elementary illustrations may help. I don't write love letters to my beloved when she is talking to me at the breakfast table; I don't beg my friend to visit me when he is already present and attentive. Some kinds of speaking depend upon absence. Indeed, in experiments conducted to determine the presence of language in animals other than humans, the basic distinction between words as reflex conditioning and words as language rests upon absence. If the word "tiger" is only used to name a tiger that is present, we have a simple conditioned reflex. But if the word (or, more precisely, the vocable) "tiger" is used appropriately in the absence of the tiger (I hate tigers, I'm afraid of tigers, etc.), then we have language. Human speech is rooted in the absence of that about which we speak.[12]

So also—all the more—is this true about prayer. I have noted that all Christian prayer is a prayer for God (and the same is true of prayer in Judaism and Islam). It is an entreaty for God to come, for God to be God, for God to be whom he has promised to be for us. We ask for that which we do not have. We ask for God because of our godlessness; we pray for God to be present because God is absent. And so we ask that God will sanctify his name, bring his kingdom, perfect his goal—because of the absence or hiddenness of these things and thus because God himself is absent, hidden, or "not yet who he will be."

We can arrive at this same conclusion if we ask what it is that we "offer" God in our praying. I believe the answer is, quite simply, our need, our lack, our emptiness. Far from constituting a barrier to prayer, this emptiness is the grounds for our addressing God. We do not pray out of our strength but out of our neediness. Jesus himself contrasted two "prayers" to make this point: "God, I thank you that I am not as other people" and "God, be merciful to me, a sinner." The first is

[12]The relationship between language and absence was noted in Susanne Langer's *Philosophy in a New Key* (Harvard, 1969), pp. 103-143. However, it is the work of contemporary French writers that has brought this concept most directly and insistently to my attention. Cf. Jacques Lacan in "Function and Field of Speech and Language," *Ecrits: A Selection*, Eng. tr. (W. W. Norton, 1977).

a prayer of strength, of one who speaks to God on the basis
of his piety and his righteousness;[13] the second is a prayer
born of need and weakness. Jesus' comment is clear: "the
second was justified." This is not a story that Jesus told to
teach us to develop proper humility; it is a statement that
clearly indicates that we truly pray when we address our neediness to God. So my uncle's embarrassed reflection on prayer
("there is no such thing as an atheist in a foxhole") turns out
to be much nearer the mark than the pious phrases that equate
true prayer with a constant sense of God's presence, because
prayer is, in the deepest sense, an emergency measure. Thus
Calvin regularly cites the words of Psalm 50, "Call upon me
in your hour of need" (vs. 15), and Augustine maintains that
"the best disposition for praying is that of being desolate, forsaken, stripped of everything."[14]

Yet it is precisely as such an emergency measure that prayer
corresponds to the basic character of our existence[15]—at least
this seems to be the view most widely attested to in biblical
literature. One illustration of this point will have to take the
place of the many that could be used here. Among the many
metaphors that are used in the Old Testament to refer to the
nature of our existence, none is more characteristic than the
term "nephesh," which is normally translated as "soul."[16] Like
most anthropological terms used in Hebrew, this word has an
anatomical reference in this case meaning "throat," "neck,"

[13]Formally there is nothing "wrong" with the prayer—or rather, the
thanksgiving—of the Pharisee. The true difficulty with the prayer is its
substitution of the "logic of scarcity" for the logic of abundance. Cf. below,
Chapters 5 and 6.

[14]The phrase of Augustine's is cited by Ellul (*Prayer and Modern Man*,
p. 105). After discussing the notion that we ought to be always equally
disposed to pray, Calvin asserts that "for the saints the occasion that best
stimulates them to call upon God is when, distressed by their own need,
they are troubled by the greatest unrest, and are almost driven out of their
senses, until faith opportunely comes to their relief" (*Institutes*, III, xx, 11
[p. 863]).

[15]Noting that prayer requires the elimination of every mask and of all
self-deception, Barth continues: "What remains when every mask falls? Obviously nothing but the privation and desire which he can only repress and
not remove" (*Church Dogmatics*, III/4, p. 98).

[16]For a lucid discussion of this and other anthropological terms in the
Old Testament, cf. Hans W. Wolff, *Anthropology of the Old Testament*, Eng.
tr. (Fortress, 1974), pp. 7-80.

or "gullet." It is used to express the way in which the throat takes in or swallows air, food, and water, and thus by extension to designate the continual neediness of human existence, which includes the need not only for air and food but for God, for God's protection and mercy. This multi-dimensional neediness is so characteristic of our existence that "nephesh" can be used, and is the term most frequently used, to designate our humanity. When we are described as "souls" in biblical literature, no dignity or religious capacity is attributed to us. Instead we are defined as needy and thus in a constant state of emergency, having to fulfill our needs to survive.

The need in focus here is the need for God, which is not one need among others—not even the greatest among several. Rather, the need for God and for his favor summarizes and comprehends all our needs—for food, for air, for comfort, for fellowship. Our need for God must not, however, be confused with a need for religion. Certainly there seem to be many people who cannot get enough of religious activity, pious feelings, and spiritual discipline. For others, even the slightest trace of such religiousness is too much. I want neither to condemn nor to condone either of these positions. My point is simply that "nephesh," the neediness of human existence, is to be vigorously distinguished from any special religious need or requirement of piety. Confusion at this point is and always has been fatal to the understanding and living out of the Christian faith.

There is, then, no religious precondition for prayer, no particular "spiritual orientation" that is necessary for prayer, no special sense of God's presence. On the contrary, the only possible basis *in us* for prayer is a sense of our need. Prayer is our directing this need toward God, our cry for God out of our godlessness. God's absence causes us to call out for God's presence.

If this idea still seems strange, we have only to recall Jesus' prayer on the cross, the prayer which, according to the Gospel of Mark, was his last utterance: "My God, my God, why hast thou forsaken me?" This protest against abandonment is the end of Jesus' ministry, the end of his life. It is precisely this end, so very different from the edifying deaths of so many—including Socrates—that moved the centurion to say, "Surely

this man was the Son of God." If we have any interest in
understanding this confession of Jesus' sonship, we must not
in any way water down or avoid the scandal of his death and
of his dying words. And if we are to have any understanding
of prayer, it must begin here, with this prayer that above all
deserves to be called "the Lord's prayer."[17]

It is the Lord's prayer first because it is through this prayer
that Jesus is made known as the Son of God, according to
Mark 15:39. It is the Lord's prayer because when Jesus uttered
these words, the veil of the temple was torn in two (Mark
15:38)—that is, the symbol of the separation of God from the
world was rent "from top to bottom." Such is the work of the
Mediator and High Priest who calls God into account, who
protests against abandonment and whose protest is "heard" in
the sundering of the barrier between God and his world.

The work of faith is not resewing this veil, re-establishing
this barrier in pious reverence of this separation. This would
be to undo Jesus' prayer, to perpetuate the comedy of those
uncomprehending people who, misunderstanding Jesus, attempted to make of his prayer a "religious act," saying, "Listen, he is calling for Elijah" (Mark 15:35). To join our prayer
with Jesus' prayer is to join in the plea for God, in the call for
God which "takes the kingdom by violence."[18] It is protesting
every barrier between ourselves and God, protesting our godlessness and godforsakenness and asking God that his name
be hallowed, his kingdom come, his goal accomplished, "on
earth as it is in heaven."

Christian prayer has no basis in our own situation and experience other than our need for God, other than our godlessness and godforsakenness. God's absence, not his presence,
is the starting point of every prayer.

[17]The reflections upon this prayer in the following paragraphs are par-
alleled by, though not directly dependent upon, the discussion of Jürgen
Moltmann in *The Crucified God*, Eng. tr. (SCM, 1974), pp. 145-153. Moltmann recognizes that these words (which are modeled on Psalm 22) may be
a subsequent interpretation of Jesus' "loud cry" but are nevertheless to be
accepted as the meaning of that cry. I find Moltmann's case persuasive at
this point, as I do his general thesis that the cross is the test and criticism
of every theology—including a "theology of prayer and praise."

[18]Cf. Romano Guardini, *The Lord's Prayer*, Eng. tr. (Pantheon, 1958),
p. 120; Ellul, *Prayer and Modern Man*, p. 161.

D. THE PROMISE OF GOD

At this point we must ask, Is our need, our godlessness a sufficient basis for prayer? I think not. It is the only basis *in us*, the only psychological precondition we have to offer, but if this were all we brought to prayer we still could not pray—not, at any rate, as Christians. But our negative basis for prayer is balanced by a positive basis for it—the promise of God.

It is God's promise that makes our prayer possible and that makes *the presumption which prayer is* possible for us. The audacity of prayer is that it makes a claim upon God, that it makes a demand upon God.[19] I have said that this demand is nothing less than that God should be God for us, that he should turn himself to us in generosity and healing. This audacity and presumption has no justification other than that it rests upon God's promise. "Let it be done to me *according to your Word*" (Luke 1:38; italics mine) is the summary of all prayer. It must be clear that we speak of God's promise, not of many promises, because basically God does not promise many things but one thing: he promises himself to his world. But this single promise enters into our history in such a way that it takes on a multiplicity of aspects, moments, and expressions. Indeed, this promise not only enters history—it is the promise which creates history.[20] It is this single promise that constitutes the history of Israel and of the Church.

To Abraham was promised a son, yet the time for raising a family passed. When at length a son was born, it was the "wrong" son—the son of Hagar. Abraham experienced hope, fulfillment, disappointment, then renewed hope when Isaac was born—only to be commanded to sacrifice the child. But even when God spared Isaac, his message was unambiguous: the hope of faith is not to be riveted upon human possibility nor even upon its apparent fulfillment. Our hope is in the promise alone, an uncalculating reliance upon God as the one

[19]Citing II Samuel 7:27, Calvin asserts, "Only that prayer is acceptable to God which is born, if I may so express it, out of such presumption of faith, and is grounded in unshaken assurance of hope" (*Institutes*, III, xx, 12 [p. 865]).

[20]For the notion that the promise creates history, cf. Jürgen Moltmann, *The Theology of Hope: On the Ground and the Implications of a Christian Eschatology*, trans. James W. Leitch (SCM, 1967), pp. 95-138 and pp. 230-303.

who promises and therefore continually draws us into a future
whose shape is obscure, perhaps even threatening, but secured
by the word of the promise "I will be with you."

Abraham was promised a land, yet in the land of promise
he was but a pilgrim, a wanderer with no abiding place. Even
when the promise appears to be fulfilled and Israel is established under David, it must once again be sacrificed. The
word of promise comes to us when we want to settle down in
history, undermining our security in the present. In this way
we are driven to recognize that the fulfillment of the promise
is still ahead, that the promise is more real than any of its
provisional fulfillments. Thus when Israel settled down in
history, the word of promise came both as a threat and a demand, for God had determined "to do a new thing." Those
religious and political institutions with which Israel made
herself an abiding place had to be sacrificed to the promise of
a new future.

This history of promise with its partial fulfillments, dis-
appointments, and renewal and enlargement of promise has
reached its climax in the history of Jesus of Nazareth, who is,
according to Paul, "the yea and amen to all God's promises"
(II Cor. 1:10). In the ministry and destiny of Jesus, then, we
discern the final clarification and ratification of all that God
has promised. Beyond this point there is no further promise,
only the coming of that which has been promised.

In the ministry and mission of Jesus, God's promise attains
a heretofore unheard-of intensity. That God will come to his
people in person is ratified in and through the person of Jesus.
In Jesus, the personal presence of God with us (and this is the
basis for confessing Jesus as the Son of God, as God and
human in one), the promises of a people, of a Davidic heir, of
a reconciliation between God and his people come to their
focal point.

At the same time these promises are enlarged to achieve a
scale, a dimension previously undreamed of. For God's promise now includes the whole of his creation, all nations united
in his covenant of grace. Beyond this, in Jesus' destiny, his
death and resurrection, is announced the new creation, a new
heaven and a new earth in which even death, the last enemy,
is overcome. In this way God's promise escapes every con-

finement, surmounting the barriers of class, of ethnic identity, of guilt (through the forgiveness of sins)—even of death.

This extension and intensification of God's promise in the person and mission of Jesus is expressed in the prayer that Jesus taught his people to pray, in the one word "Father" (Luke 11:2), in the explication of this word in Matthew, and in our liturgy "Our Father, who art in heaven." In this word is compressed the range and depth of God's promise. To call God "Father" is to call upon God "in Jesus' name," for it is to appeal to the one who is made manifest in and through Jesus.[21] Indeed, for us, there is no basis for calling God "Father" other than the command and promise, the life and death of Jesus. (I do not deny that in various ways the people of Israel could call God "Father." But we who are not blood heirs of that covenant have no basis for doing so other than this word of Jesus.)

We should clearly understand what is involved in this name and claim that is the opening of our prayer. We call upon God as our "Father" not because God is like a parent, and still less because he is like a male (rather than a female) parent. The latter notion has been rightly attacked by those who reject "paternalism" and patriarchal structures. In fact, it would not be inappropriate to address God as "Mother," considering the many "maternal" images of God in the Bible. It is far less appropriate to address God as "parent," since this all too clearly moves from personal address to categorical description. I call nobody "parent," but one "mother" and another "father," a distinction each of us must observe when we pray. We must address God, not describe him.

But many of the arguments about "paternalism" and "maternalism" suffer from a basic confusion. To call upon God as Father is so far from presupposing or validating paternalism and patriarchalism that it actually shatters them. To call upon God as Father is to call upon the God who has broken all barriers, all hierarchies, all structures—even the division between God and humanity. The God whom we call "Father" is the God who has come near to share our fate (not, therefore,

[21]"For in calling God 'Father,' we put forward the name 'Christ.' With what confidence would anyone [otherwise] address God as 'Father'?" (Calvin, *Institutes*, III, xx, 36 [p. 899]).

a paternalistic being), who has overthrown every barrier that separates us from himself and from one another (and therefore not one who legitimates the insidious barrier of patriarchalism or even matriarchalism).

To call God "Father," then, is not to claim something *about* God but to claim something *from* God. It is to claim God's promises, to call God to be near even though he seems far away. Thus there is a very real tension in the form of address in Matthew's version of this prayer: "Our Father, who art in heaven." The "Our Father" calls the near God, while the "who art in heaven" calls the distant and absent God who is summoned to be "our Father" and thus to accomplish his goal "on earth as it is in heaven." This tension between the promise of God and the absence of God is at the heart of prayer.[22]

It is in this sense that we can understand Tertullian's saying that "it is prayer that vanquishes God."[23] On the basis of God's promise, prayer calls upon the absent God (who art in heaven) to come near, to be who he has promised to be (on earth as in heaven). But on what basis do we presume thus to struggle with God (Ellul), thus to engage in the presumptuousness (Calvin) of a prayer that seeks to overcome and thus vanquish God (Tertullian)? Only on the basis of God's promise and therefore only "in Jesus' name." For it is Jesus who has taught us this presumption, the awful presumption of call-

---

[22]This tension is regularly overlooked in the text of Matthew. Yet the addition—if it is that—of the address "who art in heaven" and the conclusion of the set of petitions "as in heaven, so on earth" is striking. It is almost a complaint, a protest against God "in heaven."

"Heaven" is regularly used as a way of speaking of God in himself. So Jesus' parables are parables of "the kingdom of God" and/or "the kingdom of heaven." The complaint then is that God is God for himself (in heaven) but has not yet become God for us (on earth as in heaven). But it is the latter which he has promised.

[23]Tertullian, *On Prayer*, xxix (p. 691). "Prayer is alone that which vanquishes God." This is the theme of Ellul's *Prayer and Modern Man*, in which he describes prayer as "combat with God" (pp. 139ff.) and focuses especially upon the claim implicit in the one word "Father" (pp. 158ff.). It seems to me unfortunate, however, that Ellul relies more heavily upon the category of "command" than that of "promise" to explicate the character of prayer. Prayer is nowhere in Scripture an alien and heteronomous command, but rather arises spontaneously. Ellul is rightly suspicious of modern talk of spontaneity, but this is best corrected by way of the biblical horizon of God's promise rather than by a contest of wills in which we submit to a command.

ing God "Father." Faith consists not in pious deference to the divine majesty but in this importunate existence and presumption which, like the widow in Jesus' parable, will not cease from claiming that the judge do justice, that God be who he has promised to be (Luke 18:1-8; cf. 11:5-8).

E. THE SPIRIT OF GOD

On what basis is it possible to bridge the gulf between the absence of God and the promise of God? There is no point in denying that this chasm exists. To deny it is to render prayer impossible and to make a mockery of God's promise. We make a mockery of God's promise when we make it conform to "the way things are," when we settle for less than God. It is but a short step—if it is any step at all—from this resignation to blasphemous idolatry. If we settle for less than God, we are likely to make that "less" *into* God, and thus "God" becomes the guarantor of the way things are. This is the idolatry of those who have settled down in the land—who transform Yahweh into Baal. Under these circumstances prayer, too, ceases. Instead of asking God to be God, and thus to transform earth and heaven, we ask that heaven ratify earth.

The recognition of the chasm separating the absence of God from the promise of God, our godlessness from his mercy, is the engine that drives prayer. But having said that, we have not yet indicated how prayer is then possible. Prayer is the leap across this chasm, but how do we reach the "other side"?

Paul recognizes the impossibility of prayer when he states quite unequivocally that "we do not know how we are to pray" (Rom. 8:26). Paul is not speaking about those who have some temporary difficulty in praying, nor those who have not yet received the proper instruction, nor those who lack the proper faith. He is speaking of the Christian community, that same community which has already received the prayer of Jesus and his teaching about prayer. He says it of the whole community, in which he includes himself. If we seek to qualify our ignorance about prayer, we shall not understand it.

This not-knowing (a-gnosticism) and incapacity is grounded in the seemingly unbridgeable chasm between the absence and the promise of God. Certainly our pleas and claims are

not competent to bridge this chasm; it must be bridged—if it
is to be bridged at all—from "the other side." This, at least,
is Paul's argument in Romans 8:18-27. In our weakness, our
ignorance, we are not equal to this "combat with God" (Ellul),
we are incapable of the prayer which "vanquishes God" (Tertullian). In this unequal contest of prayer God sends his Spirit
to help us, that God may be vanquished by God. Thus with
sighings too deep for words the Spirit intercedes for us and
with us, giving us the "spirit of adoption" whereby we call
"Abba"—that is, claim the promises of God. Apart from God
the Son in the person of Jesus, we would have no right to
claim God's promises. Apart from God the Spirit, we would
not have the power to do so. This is the trinitarian foundation
for prayer.

We do well to recall this intercession of the Spirit when we
find ourselves incapable of prayer as well as when we find
ourselves all too able to pray. Our inability to pray is not a
temporary impairment or an interruption of an otherwise assured capacity for prayer; it is instead our permanent condition. But this condition is not itself a barrier to prayer, because
the Spirit intercedes for us. Thus Augustine could claim that
even wanting to pray when we cannot is itself a prayer.[24] Indeed, it is the typical character of prayer. We need not despair
of our incapacity.

On the other hand, we do need to mistrust our readiness to
pray. Glibness is a far greater obstacle to prayer than the sense
of our barrenness and God's absence. It is when prayer seems
easiest that we are in greatest danger—despite our many
words—of ceasing altogether to pray. There is more of true
prayer in a yearning sigh than in a thousand pious words.
Thus Jesus counsels us against using many words and dis-
playing competent piety (Matt. 6:7). This, then, is a proper
pastoral rule concerning prayer: beware when you find prayer
easy or think yourself accomplished in its practice; be com-
forted when you cannot pray, for the Spirit intercedes for us
and within us.

The intercession of the Spirit is an indispensable element
in the structure of prayer, for it is only by the power of God's

[24]*Letter CXXX*, x, 20 (p. 465).

THE SHAPE OF PRAYER

Spirit that prayer calls for the God who is absent to be present as he has promised, and so vanquishes God. We will return to this theme when we explore the forms of prayer.

F. COMMON PRAYER

We come now to the final fundamental element characteristic of Christian prayer—that it is always common prayer, and therefore communal prayer. We sometimes distinguish between private and public prayer, between formal and informal prayer. Such distinctions have a certain legitimacy and limited significance, but they are never fundamental to the character of prayer. Nor must we permit the use of these distinctions to lead us to suppose that there is another distinction—between individual and corporate prayer. Insofar as such a distinction exists, it separates Christian prayer from other forms of prayer. For Christian prayer is always and only corporate prayer: it is the prayer of the community or it is not prayer at all.

Seventeen hundred years ago, Clement of Alexandria pointed out this basic feature of prayer as implicit in the very form and content of the Lord's Prayer. When we pray we say, "*Our* Father," not "*My* Father." I ask not for *my* daily bread but for *our* daily bread, not that *I* will be delivered from evil but that *we* will be delivered. This is no accident of arbitrary formulation; it is the fundamental character of all prayer. We pray *only* when we pray "together." Of course we at times pray privately, silently, and hiddenly, but these prayers, insofar as they are authentic, are corporate and common prayers. Even though I pray alone on a desert island, I pray in company with all those who call upon God as Father.[25]

[25]Cyprian gives this explanation: "Before all things the teacher of peace and master of unity would not have prayer to be made singly and individually as for one who prays to pray for himself alone" (*On the Lord's Prayer*, 8 [p. 449]). So seriously does Cyprian take this principle that he considers the fomenting of strife within the community an unforgivable sin (*On the Lord's Prayer*, 23 [p. 454]).

That our prayers are corporate in character even when said in secret is stressed by Calvin: "For although prayers are individually framed . . . they do not cease to be common" (*Institutes*, III, xx, 39 [p. 902]). Barth also makes a similar point: "We are the men who are closely united, and even made brethren by their common Head and His Command, so that even in the solitude of the individual they pray and ask together, praying and asking for what is fundamentally the same thing, and doing so with and on behalf of one another" (*Church Dogmatics*, III/4, p. 102).

In prayer we are united with our sisters and brothers—indeed, with the whole of creation, which yearns in travail with us for the coming of God. We pray in the solidarity of our common godlessness and godforsakenness, and thus in solidarity with all humanity (whether pious or impious) and, indeed, with all creation.[26]

First, we pray in solidarity with all those who call upon God as Father and who therefore share with us the hope in God's promise. In this respect our prayer is the prayer of that whole community which prays "in Jesus' name." We pray, therefore, as part of the whole communion of saints: the entire people of God throughout the world and across the centuries. No matter how hidden, how silent, how private our prayer, it is prayer with the whole people of God—common prayer. The prayer of the community is not the mere aggregation of individual prayers; it is common prayer offered out of our common plight, to our common Lord, for our common hope.

Lest we seek to turn this solidarity with the community of faith into an exclusive unity, it is wise to recall again that for which we hope and therefore pray: the coming of God's kingdom, his reign and rule on earth as it is in heaven. Our hope is a hope. therefore, for the whole of creation—not for the church only. When we pray we pray with the community, but we pray on behalf of the whole of humanity, the whole of creation. God promises himself not to the church only but to the world.

The recognition of the common and communal character of prayer can serve as both a source of assurance and a warning. We can draw strength and confidence from remembering that no matter how desperate our need or sense of inadequacy, we do not stand alone when we address ourselves to God. The pharisee who prayed "I thank God I am not like other men" stood alone, though he stood in a crowd. But the publican

---

[26]That the corporate character of our prayer includes all people (not only the church) is expressed in the following way by Calvin: "Let the Christian man, then, conform his prayers to this rule in order that they may be in common and embrace all who are his brothers in Christ, not only those whom he at present sees and recognizes as such but all men who dwell on earth" (*Institutes*, III, xx, 38 [p. 901]).

who cried "Lord, be merciful to me, a sinner" was surrounded
by a host of witnesses, though he prayed in a closet.

But the nature of true prayer also reminds us of what we
may not pray for. We may not ask *this* God for anything that
separates us from our neighbor: we cannot ask for "our daily
bread" in such a way as to deny that daily bread to our neighbor. The one we call "our Father" cannot and must not be
replaced by the guardian angel of our dreams or by the deity
of our cult or sect. No prayer for private advantage can possibly be directed to the one we call "*our* Father." God's kingdom cannot come to us apart from our neighbor and still
remain God's kingdom. Thus we must constantly test our
petitions against this criterion: are they the prayers of solidarity or of division; can they be or become the prayers of the
community as a whole? How this question is answered indicates whether these prayers are directed to the Father of Jesus
(and are therefore offered in the name of Jesus) or are instead
addressed to some other deity fabricated out of our fantasy.

It is in the public prayers of the gathered community that
we are most clearly and forcefully reminded of the common
and communal character of our prayers. The formal liturgy of
the church reminds us of the unity of this community—a
unity that crosses the boundaries of time and race and language. It therefore serves as a necessary and beneficial cor-
rective to the subjective and solipsistic tendency of many of
our prayers, teaching us the true meaning of prayer "in Jesus'
name." It is for this reason that I have chosen to emphasize
public prayer, the praying we do in the hearing of others, for
it is in this communal act that we learn to pray to one who is
not *my* guardian angel but *our* Father.

In the preceding pages I have sought to indicate the most
basic features of all prayer that is prayed "in Jesus' name."
Throughout I have maintained that prayers prayed in the hearing of others have the very real capacity to lead the hearer
astray—to provoke atheism, idolatry, and superstition. It is
therefore of utmost importance that these basic features of
proper prayer be clearly kept in view and truly exemplified in
the praying that we do, whether in private or in public. For
this reason I offer a brief review of these features:

1. *Prayer is addressed to God.*

In our prayer we address ourselves to God, not to the congregation (in pastoral prayers) or to any other hearer. Failure to observe this simple rule is astonishingly widespread in our churches and is the greatest single factor in producing the practical atheism that finds prayer meaningless or "therapeutic." But beyond this is the further question, to which God do we address our prayers? That our prayers even in our churches—or perhaps especially there—are directed to some other god than Jesus' Father produces a superstitious, pagan, and idolatrous Christianity.

2. *Prayer is an asking for God.*

That in prayer we are fundamentally asking for God to come to us and be with us, for God to be God and therefore our God, is clear from considering the meaning of the first three "petitions" of the Lord's Prayer, summarized by the "maranatha" of the earliest Christian community. In prayer, therefore, we do not ask for many things but for one thing. When we fail to discern this unity of our plea, we transform God into a tooth fairy, but when we observe this basic unity our prayer consists of the presumption to demand nothing less than God himself.

3. *Prayer is grounded in the absence of God.*

We pray for God's coming because of God's absence. No special religious sense or feeling of "divine presence" is prerequisite to prayer. On the contrary, it is precisely in our godlessness and godforsakenness that we call for God to come, for God to be God, and therefore join our prayers with that of Jesus, who cried, "My God, my God, why hast thou forsaken me?" Prayer is not an act of piety but the crying out of need.

4. *Prayer is holding God to his promise.*

What right do we who are godless have to demand that God come to us? Our sole right to the audacity and presumption of prayer that "takes the kingdom by violence" is the promise of God. This promise attains clarity in the person and destiny of Jesus, which authorizes us to call upon God as "our Father" and thus to claim that promise for ourselves. This is the objective basis for the prayer that "vanquishes God."

5. *Prayer is possible because of God's Spirit.*

It is the Spirit alone who gives our otherwise impotent and incompetent prayer the power to accomplish its aim, to lay hold of God's promise even in our godlessness. We have reason to be confident, therefore, even when we know that we cannot pray, but we also have reason to be especially on guard when we feel all too able to pray. When we pray in the power of our own piety, we do not truly pray at all.

6. *Prayer is common prayer.*

The Spirit who enables us to pray by praying in and through us is also the Spirit who makes us one. Our prayer is Christian prayer only to the extent that it is also corporate prayer, the prayer of the community in solidarity with all humanity, with the whole groaning creation. Thus we pray to *our* Father for *our* bread and for the accomplishment not of our desire but of his kingdom.

By attending to these basic characteristics of Christian prayer, we will be able to distinguish in our prayers that which authentically testifies to faith from that which is born of or produces atheism, idolatry, and superstition. In this way we will be able to discern whether and to what extent we truly pray "in Jesus' name."

CHAPTER TWO
The Forms of Prayer

Thus far I have sketched the basic structure of prayer but have not discussed its variations. In the next few pages I will describe three of the basic types of prayer that constitute the common prayer of the congregation. In this discussion there will be one crucial omission: the so-called prayer of confession. I omit this prayer because it belongs to a different liturgical complex, a sequence different from the sequence of prayer and praise that is the subject of this book. Viewed simply as prayer, it has the same features that we have been and will be discussing, but it has its own distinctive sequence of repentance and absolution. This sequence is every bit as fundamental as the sequence of prayer and praise and deserves its own full-length treatment in a subsequent discussion. Also omitted from consideration here is the *epiklesis*, which is the call for God to come to us through the words or objects (water, wine, bread) of our worship. Examination of this call properly belongs to a discussion of word and sacrament, and so exceeds the scope of this book.

In what follows, then, I will limit my discussion to three types of prayer: invocation, petition, and intercession. Discussing these types of prayer will enable us to summarize the elements of the structure of prayer while continuing to reflect upon some of the problems we have with prayer—especially the matter of the answering of prayer.

Two other activities sometimes described as prayer find no place here: meditation and contemplation. They are left out first because they have no public, corporate, or liturgical expression, and our aim here is to understand the outward expressions of prayer. The second reason for omitting them is that I am not sure that they belong under the heading of prayer at all. At best they may be understood as "accessories" to prayer, as preparation for prayer or, in certain cases, as the goal of some prayers. But they do not seem to be prayer itself.[1] In any case, there are those who may speak far more competently than I about these activities, which are outside my competence as a theologian.

We will focus, then, on three basic types of prayer, which can be briefly defined. Invocation is the call to God in the person of the Spirit to be present with us to enable us to pray. Petitionary prayer is the expression of our many needs to him from whom we ask "our daily bread." And intercessory prayer is the articulation of the need of others as though it were our own. Discussing these three forms of prayer will help us see still more clearly the appropriate character of that prayer which we pray "in Jesus' name."

A. INVOCATION

Beginning our common prayer is the invocation, the summoning of the Spirit of God. This is not only the beginning of our common prayer; it is its most comprehensive expression. All prayer is summarized by the prayer that calls for God's presence in and through us.

In order to understand the nature and importance of the invocation, we must clearly separate it from the "call to worship," with which it is sometimes confused. The call to worship is an address directed to the congregation that announces the beginning of the corporate worship of those assembled and invites them to engage in that worship. The invocation is addressed to God. When these two are confused, often by the habit of bowing at the call to worship, the whole character of prayer—not only the invocation—is destroyed. Such confusion is not at all likely in the more formal worship services of liturgically oriented communities of faith, but the confu-

---

[1]Barth maintains not only that these are not prayer but that they are an evasion of prayer (*Church Dogmatics*, III/4, p. 97). Similarly, Ellul dismisses these from his consideration of prayer (*Prayer and Modern Man*, pp. 25ff.). While these delimitations and exclusions are, to my mind, too harshly formulated by Barth and especially by Ellul, their position seems to me to be essentially correct at this point.

sion is astonishingly and embarrassingly widespread in the
less formal worship of many mainline and "conservative"
Protestant congregations. In these churches the most important "liturgical reform" that can be imagined is the careful
and complete distinction between those words addressed to
God and those addressed to the congregation. The simple
enforcement of this distinction will go far in clarifying the
character of prayer in and for the congregation.

We begin our worship with the invocation because it is the
indispensable basis for that worship. We have seen that we are
in fact incapable of true prayer apart from the intercession of
the Spirit. In our godlessness we lack the power to hold God
to his promise, to claim this promise for ourselves. Our condition is one of lack or need rather than fullness and power.
This is, after all, why we pray. But the Spirit of God em-
powers and enlivens our prayers, infusing them with the
strength to "vanquish" God. It is in and through this empowerment of the Spirit that we are able to cry "Abba" and thus
to make the claim and demand upon God to be "our Father."
The invocation, then, is a calling for God, for God as this
Spirit to make it possible for us to pray. If our worship is to
be a worship of prayer, it requires the presence and empowerment of this Spirit. This is, of course, all the more true if
our worship is also to be an offering of praise and thanksgiving, as we shall see in a later chapter.

The invocation of God the Spirit to come to us and em-
power us is the presupposition and precondition of our prayers
in another way as well. I have indicated that our prayer, insofar as it is Christian prayer, must also be common prayer—
the prayer of God's people—and not a collection of individual
and idiosyncratic prayers. But it is the Spirit who constitutes
the unity of this community, establishing cohesion and co-
herence. If our prayers are to be joined with the prayers of
those from whom we are separated by time, language, culture,
and interest, and so become the prayer of the community, the
Spirit must accomplish this unity.

The invocation is, therefore, the true and indispensable
beginning of our common prayer. Beyond this we may also

say that the invocation contains and summarizes all our prayer. As we have seen in the preceding chapter, our prayer is fundamentally a plea for God to come to us. No matter how many petitions we may make, our prayer is a prayer for God's coming, for God's rule and reign, for the accomplishment of God's purpose. Thus we pray "your name be hallowed, your kingdom come, your will be done—on earth as it is in heaven." Our prayer is a call to the absent God to come to us as he has promised. And this is precisely the structure and explicit content of a prayer of invocation, which asks God to be not alien and distant and threatening but present as empowering and enlivening and therefore as Spirit. To pray for the Spirit is to pray for God to come to us as he has promised to come "in the last days"—through the sending of that Spirit which is the gift par excellence of the coming God (Joel 2:28; Zech. 4:6; Isa. 44:3; 63:14).

Thus the prayer of invocation is both the beginning of our prayers and the summary of them. But it is not the only prayer we make. By virtue of the presence and power of this Spirit we go on to the diverse and specific prayers of petition and intercession, to which we now turn.

B. PETITION

Our common prayer is fundamentally a prayer for the coming of God. Precisely as this plea and claim, however, it is at the same time composed of a series of pleas and claims that are particular and limited. For the coming of God, the rule and reign of God, is not something abstract or "general." The transformation for which we yearn on the basis of God's promise is not a transformation that is only "inward" or "spiritual" or "supernatural"; it is a transformation that includes the specifics of our everyday existence. This is the meaning of the insistent plea of the Lord's Prayer—"as in heaven, so on earth." This is the plea that God reign not only "in heaven," only in principle, only "in himself," only "supernaturally," but also concretely, specifically, manifestly, and thus "on earth."

1. Our Daily Bread

It is thus not an alien or fundamentally new theme that is introduced by the petition "Give us this day our daily bread."[2] At first this petition seems incongruous in its setting. After such weighty matters as God's name, kingdom, and purpose and before the no-less-weighty matters of sin, temptation, and evil stands this plea for "everyday bread." Some people may be scandalized at this mundane, worldly, and self-centered intrusion into an otherwise high-minded, altruistic, and thus "spiritual" setting. The theologian Origen, for example, argued (scarcely two hundred years after Jesus' death) that this petition could not have its apparent meaning but must instead

---

[2]The meaning of this petition has been the subject of considerable debate in the history of the church. In the text of Matthew and Luke, the object of the petition is our "epi-ousion"—bread. The adjective, odd and obscure, has been made to bear the meaning of "super-natural" or "super-substantial," though modern commentators agree that it must mean "daily" or, perhaps, "nourishing" or "sufficient." Beyond this, the texts differ: Matthew has "give to us for tomorrow," while Luke has "give to us each day" (or, possibly, "according to the day"). While translation is extremely difficult here, the general meaning appears not to be distorted by the rendering "give us today our daily bread." (For a discussion of the textual difficulties, see Lohmeyer, "Our Father," pp. 134-159.)

The obscurities of the text itself, together with the theological predispositions of the interpreters, have resulted in considerable divergence of opinion. Origen completely excludes the possibility that this petition could refer to something so mundane as everyday needs like bread. "Everyone therefore who asks God for earthly and little things disregards the command to ask for heavenly and great things from God who knows not to grant anything earthly or little" (On Prayer, XVI, 2 [p. 272]). Origen then supplies "knowledge" as the meaning of the petition (p. 300).

Augustine seems to agree with Origen in his commentary on Our Lord's Sermon on the Mount, VII, 27 [p. 42]), though he permits the inclusion of daily needs and the sacrament so long as priority is given to the Word of God as that which gives us knowledge of God. This order of priority is then reversed in his Letter CXXX, in which he stresses "temporal blessings" and permits the extension of this to include the sacrament but omits any mention of the Word.

The sobriety of the later Augustine comes to dominate subsequent discussions, including that of Aquinas, who stresses that we may ask here for whatever we need, though not either for excess nor for that which can come to "ill-use" (Summa Theologica, II, II, Q. 83, Art. 4, p. 1540). Similarly, Calvin supposes that this petition may include "not only food and clothing but also . . . everything God perceives to be beneficial to us" (Institutes, III, xx, 44 [p. 908]). Finally, Wesley's formulation seems to be admirably precise: "By bread we understand all things needful whether for our souls or bodies" (Sermon XXI, Wesley's Standard Sermons, p. 440).

have a spiritual, philosophical meaning; he supposed it must therefore refer to God's word, which alone is proper "meat and drink" to those who have set their sights upon the great and spiritual things. Other theologians, like Tertullian a few decades earlier and Aquinas nearly a millennium later, have included in the meaning of this petition the sacramental bread of the Eucharist, as if to mitigate somehow the crude materialism and secularity of this plea for ordinary, everyday bread.

Of course we cannot quarrel with the *extension* of the meaning of everyday bread to include eucharistic bread, or even the bread of God's word and promise. The difficulty arises when these "religious" or "spiritual" interpretations are no longer governed by the entirely secular and everyday reality of our actual need for bread. Then an entirely false and arrogant "spiritualism" separates itself from, and substitutes itself for, the genuine worldliness of faith. What we must realize is that contemplative theologians are not the only ones faced with this temptation, as our public prayers prove. For how often in these prayers do we ask God to *help* us get what we need rather than to *give* us what we need? (Help us to see your will, help us to know, help us to work hard enough to earn a living. . . .) This psychologizing and spiritualizing of prayer rests upon a complete misunderstanding, one that makes prayer a device for self-instruction, a kind of pious pep rally, an exercise in auto-suggestion. Such nonsense does not meet even the first condition of prayer—it is not directed to God, and cannot be.

We cannot evade the crass materialism and crude secularity of this petition—"Give us today our daily bread." Undoubtedly many noble and holy sages have taught their followers to ignore the basic and mundane necessities of life, to try to live on a higher plane. It would be folly to deny the nobility of these proposals or of those who made them, but Jesus and his teachings do not belong among them. For Jesus, broken bodies and empty bellies are the antithesis of God's reign; he embodies God's rule through healing broken bodies, filling empty bellies, and conducting himself in such a way that he is called a "winebibber and glutton."

And so he instructs his followers to ask God for whatever they need and to pray, "Give us today our daily bread." This is not a departure from but a further intensification of those

petitions which precede it: hallow your name, bring your kingdom, accomplish your aim—"as in heaven, *so also on earth*."
That precisely in doing these things God should also meet
our everyday needs follows necessarily from the very name of
the one to whom we pray. For our prayers are not addressed
to an anonymous supreme being but to the one we are permitted—even commanded—to call "Father."

I have said that when we pray we basically ask only for *one*
thing—that God be God, our God. Because the one thing we
pray for is *that* one thing, we therefore ask for "many things,"
for God's coming means that the hungry are fed, the captives
freed, the blind made to see, the lame made to walk, the dead
made alive. Thus we ask for bread, and if for bread then for
all other things that we need. This single petition is refracted
in many petitions, just as light is refracted by a prism into a
variety of colors. Our common prayer, then, is not only an
invocation but, precisely because of the one who is thus in-
voked, a series of many petitions: for food, for clothing and
shelter, for companionship, for healing, for justice, for liberty.
We are permitted to ask God for whatever we need, and lest
we doubt it, we are actually commanded to do so: "When you
pray, say . . . give us today our daily bread."

2. Our Need

The appropriateness of the petitionary prayers that we offer in
public and in common must be judged from the double standpoint of our need and God's promise. We need to examine the
character of our petitions from each of these standpoints before we turn to the question that most naturally arises from
the consideration of petition—namely, the question of "unanswered" prayer.

That we ask for our daily bread means that we ask for what
we need. As we have already seen, our life is one of lack and
need. This is what is meant when in the Old Testament we
are called "nephesh"—soul. It is this neediness out of which
we turn to God and to which we give voice in our petitions.

Appropriate petitions, then, give voice to our actual needs.
In a consumer society it is increasingly difficult to identify
real needs and to distinguish these from the fabricated and
imaginary "needs" created in the interest of greater consump-

tion. We are almost completely confused about what we need, and even about what we truly desire, a confusion that breeds bondage to things which, in truth, we neither need nor desire. This, in turn, breeds the sense of emptiness in the midst of plenty so characteristic of modern industrialized societies. It is tempting to apply a radical remedy to this malaise, to insist that our need is basically a need for God and that the rest is unimportant. Though this is in many respects true, it would render our petition for daily bread meaningless and would encourage a false spiritualizing of prayer—a spiritualizing utterly alien to the character of biblical faith in general and to the proclamation of Jesus in particular.

Despite our bewilderment about our need, it is nonetheless appropriate to express these needs in our petition. This places a particular burden of discernment upon those who are called upon to pray publicly, whether at home, in the hospital, or in church in the "pastoral prayer" of our common worship. What, after all, are our most basic needs? For what do we yearn? This must not be psychologized or spiritualized in such a way as to evade the physical, emotional, and material needs of our life. We need nourishing food, warmth and shelter, healthy bodies and sane minds. We need strength and courage, and rest from our work; we need to be touched and held, to have companions with whom we can share joy and sorrow. We also yearn for justice and liberty, for dignity and respect. For all of these things we may pray. They are to us "daily bread."

But we do not need a fancier church building, a larger church membership, a new fur coat, victory for our football team, or the fear or adulation of our peers. A great deal of what passes for prayer is frivolous, springing from our utter confusion about what we need. Far too many prayers have as their model a letter to Santa Claus, the ramblings of a greedy and bewildered child. How long will it be before Christians outgrow the pagan cult of Santa Claus and the tooth fairy? It is little wonder that adults sometimes think that the church is for gullible children.

In admonishing his disciples to pray, Jesus assures them that God, like a father, will not give stones to his children who ask for bread. Our situation is quite different: we are like children who ask for stones instead of bread. Many of our prayers are petitions for things that are not only unnecessary but destructive. Often the "problem" with "unanswered prayer" is that we have received bread when we sought stones. We ask to be let alone and are confronted instead with our neighbor's need. We seek to be tranquilized and are awakened to pain and joy. We pray to the great magician and are answered instead by the crucified God.

Alas, it is not always so. People have often assured me that their prayers have been answered, but the evidence that they too often supply is that they have received the stones they asked for. They have asked to be rich and fat and lazy and smug (though not in so many words), and have received full measure. Churches have prospered on a firm foundation of such infantile superstition. Husbands and wives have been reconciled to relationships destructive of any human feeling. The rich have had their consciences eased. One of Saint Augustine's aphorisms is appropriate here: "God often withholds in mercy what he grants in anger."[3] Another older saying is also appropriate: those whom the gods would destroy they first make mad. To avoid asking for the wrong thing, we should pray as Jesus prayed—not my will but thine be done. We should use this approach not because we may not claim what we need from God, but because we are bewildered about what we need, and should rely not on ourselves but upon God's promise.

3. God's Promise

In our prayers of petition we ask for our daily bread and thus for whatever we need. This simple request is made complex by our bewilderment over what we need, a confusion from which we are rescued by this further definition: we pray for what God promises. It is in the light of this promise that we, for the first time, see ourselves clearly, and thus see our needs clearly.

Above all God has promised to come to us, with healing and in mercy, to be Emmanuel, God with us. And lest we be confused about what this might mean, he has come to us "in

---

[3]See, for example, *NPF*, I, *Letter CXXX*, *Letter XIV*, and *passim*. Cf. Aquinas, *Summa Contra Gentes*, III, ii, 96.

advance" through Jesus, in his life and mission and destiny. We therefore pray for his coming and for all that is consistent with his coming. His single promise is faceted to reflect its true radiance. God does not come in the single note of the absolute but in the symphony of a new heaven and new earth. Our petitions are therefore as diverse as that hoped-for transformation. Where there is death, we pray for life; where there is hunger, we pray not only for nourishment but for the banquet; where there is isolation, we pray for the fellowship of all creation; where there is imprisonment, we pray for liberty; where there is oppression, we pray for justice. . . . All of this is entailed in God's promise of himself to his creation. It is by way of this promise that we discover, if we had not learned it before, that we need justice and freedom, that we need not only enough to eat but enough to share, that we need joy, not merely the cessation of sorrow. In these way, then, God's promise makes our petitions even bolder and broader than if we were left alone to apply the criterion of what we need.

But if God's promise is more generous than our need, it also imposes on us a clarifying and in some ways severe restriction. I have said that our petitions may include all that is consistent with the coming of that God who is made manifest in Jesus—but our petitions are appropriate if they claim *only* that which is consistent with the coming of *this* God.

How many of our petitions are actually grounded in the secret or open wish that *this* God never appear? How are we to reconcile our petitions with the one to whom they are made? We pray for fur coats while our neighbors have rags, for even fuller bellies while the children of our sisters have bellies bloated with hunger. We pray for more sumptuous church buildings while the poor and aged shiver in forgotten attics, for a new pulpit while the gospel is silenced in lands near and far. We pray for security from the mutinous resentment of the third world. Such prayers are openly defiant and contemptuous of God. That they are often cloaked in piety only makes their utter idolatry and blasphemy more apparent. Do we seriously imagine that we can pray in Jesus' name for success in war, for enrichment and esteem in a structure that robs the poor?

But the disease goes even deeper than these indications

would suggest. It is difficult to hear but it is nonetheless clear that God's promise is not that we shall find the resources to come to terms with our situation but that the situation itself will be utterly transfigured. Thus we are promised not that we will find the strength to die complacently, but that death will be destroyed; not that we will adjust to pain, but that pain will be overcome; not that religion will flourish, but that it will end; not that the church will be victorious, but that God will triumph; not that fewer will starve, but that all will be fed; not that the blind will compensate, but that they will see; not that the lame will adjust, but that they will walk and run and leap. But our prayers are often for adjustment, acceptance, compensation! If the previous prayers indicated an open contempt for God, these prayers reveal a debilitating timidity, a secret refusal to believe that God can or will do what he promises. Having ceased to hope for God, we ask instead for consolation.

We mask our timidity as maturity, renouncing the childish petitions of our infancy because we know that God will not give us a bicycle or cure our cold. It is no doubt important to learn that prayer ought not to be frivolous or self-seeking. But we take this "principle" of maturity still further, no longer expecting God to heal or to liberate and asking instead for vague psychic resources so that we can change what can be changed and accept what is unalterable (Niebuhr). Lurking behind this maturity is secret despair, a refusal to hope. For have we not also forgotten to expect God himself, his reign, his transformation of heaven and also of earth, the resurrection of the dead, the abolition of dark and death and sorrow? And if we no longer expect these things, do we any longer expect anything at all? And if we no longer expect anything, do we not then become afraid to name our need, our longing? As a consequence, we become unconscious of these needs, becoming merely irritable, merely impatient, no longer sure of what we want or need. Is this maturity—or is it in fact senility?

We pass off this senility as wisdom; indeed, in our enlightenment we have determined to be wiser than God. We exchange the resurrection of the body for the immortality of the soul. Instead of a new heaven and earth we ask for transport from the old earth to the old heaven. Or perhaps we give up both earth and heaven (undoubtedly "mythological" conceptions) and seek in prayer only a soporific for our troubled spirits, a pious sedative from the cosmic tranquilizer. But what is the advantage of this over drinking beer and watching TV? It is no wonder people see no need to pray, especially those who can afford six packs and a color set.

No, prayer has nothing to do with rendering us unconscious of our need, our pain, our yearning, our alienation. Prayer is precisely the articulation of this need and longing, not only in general terms but also in concrete detail. Prayer names this need and longing to the one who for our sakes became needy (II Cor. 8:9) and godforsaken, to the one who shares in our abandonment ("who became sin who knew no sin," as Paul puts it in II Corinthians 5:21), to the one who promises us himself. Thus we pray for what we need—not because God is the great Shopping Center in the Sky, but because he has entered deeply into our need, has become needy for our sakes (shall we then cover up this need?), and because we know and cling to what he has promised.

4. "Unanswered" Prayer

It is at this point, when we are most bold and authentic in our prayers, that we are met head-on with the implacable silence of God. People sometimes speak of "the problem of unanswered prayer," but that is altogether too mild a term for what we encounter here. Most often this "problem" is met on a trivial level—on the level of a complete misunderstanding of our need and God's promise. But when we clearly perceive these two things, we confront for the first time the deep and inescapable absurdity of prayer.

We pray for God's coming. Two thousand years after Jesus proclaimed his coming, the church still prays "Lord, come." These two thousand years stand as an ironclad argument against the so-called efficacy of prayer. We must be utterly clear on this point, because if we in any way mitigate or erase this scandal we shall do so only at the cost of a complete renunciation of faith in this God and his promise.

That we have lost all sense of perspective in this matter is evident from the way in which "the problem of unanswered prayer" is frequently raised. To put it simply, we balk if we don't get our way about the healing of a relative or the growth of our congregation, but shrug off the "delay" of the Parousia. Nothing could better show how utterly ridiculous we have become. We swallow elephants whole and gag on gnats. No matter what specific requests we make, the one prayer we always pray—"your kingdom come"—is the one unanswered prayer. If this petition were answered, we would no longer feel the very real brokenness and despair which is our regular lot and which, in particular cases and situations, raises "the problem of unanswered prayer."

There are times when we ask for what we need, when we truly pray on the basis of God's promise. And there are times (and all Christians experience this) when we receive what we need—not only in general but in particular. If this is what we mean by prayer being answered, then I do not by any means wish to deny that our petitions are sometimes granted. The place to discuss that, however, is in the description of praise and thanksgiving, because it is in those activities that we respond to what we have been given. When prayer is answered, prayer ceases and praise begins. But there are also times when we truly pray for what we need on the basis of what God has promised and do *not* receive what we need. Despite the assurance of Jesus, we ask for bread and receive stones. Of course, we often pray confusedly for things we do not need or on some basis other than God's promise, a problem we have already discussed. But undoubtedly we sometimes pray truly for what we need—and are met with silence. We must not erase or mitigate this difficulty, because it plainly exists. We need especially to beware of attempts to make excuses for God in this matter. We must not invoke the "mysterious ways of God" as though we were utterly ignorant of God's will, as though God were an "oriental despot" of inscrutable intentions. We know God's intentions perfectly well; we have heard the Gospel.

We must not speak lightly here of God's testing of us. In the same prayer in which we ask God to bring the kingdom and to give us bread, we also ask that God not put us to the test ("lead us not into temptation"). It is true that the pain and loss of "unanswered" prayer does in fact "put us to the test";

indeed, the presence of suffering and the power of death contradict our prayer and God's promise. The threat and fact of evil bring us to the point of a temptation that we cannot withstand: the temptation that we should cease to hope, cease to claim God's promise for ourselves and our world. And so our prayer concludes with this petition: that we not be put to the test. To this the text of Matthew adds, "but deliver us from evil." This is indeed what must occur if we are not to be put to a test which we cannot withstand—that evil be abolished. Augustine rightly notes of this petition that it is the summary of all our petitions.[4]

Accordingly, we must not speak here of being tempted by God, for we pray, "Lead us not into temptation, but deliver us from evil." We ask this, let us remember, because we are commanded to ask it, and because the same promise attaches to this petition as to the others: "Ask and it will be given you"

---

[4]It is important to note that the text of the Lord's Prayer in Luke ends with "and lead us not into temptation" (or the test, or trial). The position of this petition suggests that it is not only one (or even the last) in a series of petitions, but the conclusion of that series. It does not merely "dangle" at the end but precisely confronts the problem of all prayer. It does this not by giving an explanation for unanswered prayer but by asking, claiming, and demanding of God that we not be put to the test, that our prayer as a whole not be shattered upon the silence and absence of God.

In this connection we may recall Jesus' words to his disciples in Gethsemane: "Watch and pray, that you may not enter into temptation" (Mark 14:38, and parallels). His point here is not that the disciples may fall asleep, but that their hope and faith may shatter upon the fate of Jesus—upon the silence and absence of God in the godforsakenness of Jesus.

It is therefore to be understood as a continuation and expansion of this petition (and *not* as a new petition) when the Matthean version adds, "But deliver us from evil" (Calvin, *Institutes*, III, xx, 35 [p. 898]). The connection between temptation and evil that characterizes this Matthean version is echoed in James 1:13: "Let no one say when he is tempted, 'I am tempted by God'; for God cannot be tempted with evil and he himself tempts no one." This somewhat murky assertion stands in the context of a general admonition to stand fast in faith and hope and so in prayer (Jas. 1:5; cf. 5:14-18). Thus the assertion of James may be read as a gloss upon the Matthean version of this petition. We are justified, then, in considering "and lead us not into temptation but deliver us from evil" as a single petition.

It is appropriate to apply Augustine's words concerning "deliver us from evil" to the petition as a whole: "This petition which stands last in the Lord's prayer is so comprehensive that a Christian, in whatsoever affliction he may be placed, may in using it give utterance to his groans, find vent for his tears—may begin with this petition, go on with it, and with it conclude his prayer" (*Letter CXXX*, xii, 22 [p. 466]).

(Luke 11:9). It is dangerous—indeed, it is blasphemous—to make excuses for God. Our task is not to "justify the ways of God to man" (Milton), but to ask God to "justify us to himself" (Luther) as he has promised.

We must not conceal from ourselves the fact of prayer that is unanswered. We must acknowledge that God's promise to us is unfulfilled both in general and, therefore, in particular. It is when we are confronted particularly and concretely with the absence of that for which we yearn that we come closest to the heart and center of prayer. Here we are faced with the remarkable fact that *prayer is not a stratagem for getting what we want. It is simply a holding of God to his promise* in which we are repeatedly confronted with the pain and loss that we feel when we permit ourselves to yearn for a kingdom that has not yet come. It is precisely in the tension of this unfulfilled promise, of this unanswered prayer, of this absence of the one who has promised to be with us, that our prayer fully becomes the prayer of those who follow Jesus. Here, if we do not distract ourselves with easy and trivial assurances, with incompetent excuses for God, we shall truly begin to pray. Here we learn what it means to pray for the coming of God's kingdom. Here we find no consolation for our loss, our yearning, our cry; instead we find comfort—in the proper sense, meaning "strengthening"—which comes from knowing that our prayers join with those of the one who cried, "My God, my God, why have you forsaken me?" Thus we truly pray "in Jesus' name" and "for Jesus' sake."

And so we pray for what we need, but not based on a calculation about what we are likely to get. No such calculation could possibly justify prayer—it only renders prayer superstitious or timid. We ask for what we need because God has promised to meet our need not only in particulars but in totality, not only in general but in detail. This is what it means to pray, "as in heaven, so also on earth"; to pray, "Give us this day our daily bread"; to pray, "Lead us not into temptation, but deliver us from evil."

C. INTERCESSION

We ask for fulfillment not only of our needs, but also of the needs of our neighbors, our sisters and brothers. As the Spirit intercedes for us, with us, and in us, so we also intercede for our neighbor. In this intercession we give voice to our neighbor's pain and brokenness, to the cry of our world for God. And we do this not only in general but also in particular detail. Here we will briefly explore the basis for doing so, and the implications for the character of our prayer.

We must be careful not to misapprehend the essential character of intercession. Intercessory prayer is not some extra or dispensable sort of prayer; it is essential to the character of prayer itself that it be offered not only on my behalf but on my neighbor's behalf as well. That all prayer is intercessory prayer is already implicit in the claim that the one to whom prayer is addressed is not "my Father" but "our Father." Of course I may at times address God as *my* God, but this is only possible—God is only my God—because he is *our* Father. That we pray for one another is the necessary consequence of the communal and corporate character of Christian prayer. Thus, when Christian communities are enjoined to "pray for one another" (Eph. 6:18), we are not confronted with a view of prayer any different from that which is already present in Jesus' command: "When you pray, say, 'Our Father.'" Similarly, when we pray for "our daily bread," we pray not only for what we need but for our neighbor's need as well. If we pray at all "in Jesus' name," we of necessity pray for our neighbor. In short, intercessory prayer is at the heart of our common prayer.[5] What is true of petition, then, is also true of intercession: the appropriateness of our prayer has two sides, two tests. When we pray for our neighbor, we are guided by our neighbor's actual need and by God's promise.

In intercession we do not give voice to our neighbor's need out of altruism. I do not know whether there are altruistic people or motives, but whatever place altruism may have in our lives and characters, it has no place in prayer. We pray for our neighbor because his or her need is finally no different

---

[5]There can scarcely be any improvement made on Cyprian's position here: "One should thus pray for all, even as He Himself bore us all in one" (*On the Lord's Prayer*, 8 [p. 449]). He further stresses: "We reasonably, who ought to be like God our Father who maketh his sun to rise upon the good and the bad, and sends rain upon the just and the unjust, so pray and ask by the admonition of Christ as to make our prayer for the salvation of all men" (*On the Lord's Prayer*, 17 [p. 952]).

from our own. And because we know that we can never get
what we need alone or apart from the groaning of creation and
the cry of our neighbor. For what we need, if we understand
the claims of the New Testament correctly, is not "the salvation of my soul" but the resurrection of the dead: not an
escape from the old earth to the old heaven but "a new heaven
and a new earth." We need God to come to reign in mercy
over his whole creation. Apart from this we have no hope
whatever, no hope that can be based upon the message, mission, life, and destiny of Jesus. If we substitute this hope and
faith for the cult of the cosmic tooth fairy, our prayer is directed to one who is not my guardian angel but the Lord of
heaven and earth, not "the lover of my soul" but the one who
so loved *the world* that he gave his only son. Precisely because
we pray for what we need we pray for that which our neighbor
needs as well.

To say this much is already to say that I must see my neighbor in the light of God's promise if I am to intercede on her
behalf to this God. It is all too easy to overlook our neighbor's
need, to become accustomed or resigned to the suffering of
others. After all, that people die of starvation is a simple law
of economics and geography. That we are subject to diseases
is a law of nature. That millions die needlessly is "the way it
is." That people are oppressed by cruel, rapacious govern-
ments is "the way it's always been." All of this is certainly
true, and thus, in itself, is not so awfully outrageous—*unless*
we have reason to believe that this is not the way it is to be.
When justice is promised, injustice becomes an outrage. When
the banquet of plenty is promised, starvation is intolerable.
When the resurrection of the dead is announced, the agony of
diseased death is an obscenity. When the reign of the Prince
of Peace is proclaimed, the "necessity" of militarism, impe-
rialism, and the threat of war is unacceptable madness.

In the light cast by God's promise, the need of our neighbor
cries out to God for an accounting. Insofar as we claim and
cling to the promise, we give voice to that cry. The pain and
agony of my neighbor does not give rise to the so-called the-
odicy question; it gives rise to prayer, to the call for God. The
agony of creation does not give us occasion to attempt to justify God, to make excuses for him; it calls for God to justify

himself and us on the basis of what has been promised. It is because and only because we believe God's promises that the agony of our neighbor is not a matter of indifference to us.[6]

Again, what is true of petition is also true of intercession: we are concerned here with our need and God's promise not only in general but in particular. Thus we are concerned not with some vague spiritual need of our neighbor, but with our neighbor's actual and physical need. If I am to intercede for my neighbor, I must take seriously his specific needs. Of course, all of our needs are summarized in our need for God, for his rule and presence and, therefore, for his coming. But this most basic need is not a different need separate from or co-existing with our need for bread, for companionship, for justice. Our need for God is not some spooky additional need that we place atop our "other" needs. It is as we pray and because we pray for God's coming that we pray for "our daily bread." If we understand this clearly, then we will not be tempted to bypass our neighbor's actual and specific need by focusing on some "other" need we may have in mind.

We are keenly tempted to substitute something else for our neighbor's need. This temptation is most evident at those times when someone specifically asks us to pray for them in their particular need. The situation that comes most immediately to mind is one that almost every pastor and priest has confronted many times: a person who is dying pleads with us to pray that she will not die. We know perfectly well that her disease is incurable, and we also have a proper sense of the overwhelming improbability of a "miraculous cure." What are we to do? The overwhelming temptation is to pray for something like "the presence of God" to give "comfort, strength, and reassurance" to this person. I am not saying that such a prayer is always inappropriate, but we should think about what has happened in it: we have substituted what *we* need for what our neighbor needs. Our prayer for "peace of mind" is then just another pious way of passing by on the other side.

What is it that can lead us, even though we have the best of motives, to do precisely what we intend not to do? How is

---

[6]Moltmann's reflections upon apathy and passion seem to me to be particularly apt here. See *Passion for Life: A Messianic Lifestyle*, Eng. tr. (Fortress, 1978), pp. 19-26 and *passim*.

our solicitude transformed into betrayal? At work here, I believe, is a subtle and specific form of unbelief that is revealed when we ask ourselves this question: To what extent is this prayer based upon a calculation of how we suppose God is or is not likely to answer our prayers? We have calculated (perhaps quite rightly) that the person we are praying for will die. Of course we run some risk in such a calculation, but let us suppose that it is exact and conclusive. Still, what has this calculation to do with prayer? Prayer is not asking for what we are likely to get; it is asking for what we need and for what God promises. Prayer is based not on confidence (that is, an extrapolation of what is likely), but on hope or, as Paul says, hope against hope (Rom. 4:18). Our neighbor cries out for breath, for time, for life. To our neighbor and to us God promises healing, life, an end to sorrow and separation. Why, then, do we fear to pray for these things?

We fear, of course, that God will not answer our prayer, will not do what he has promised. Indeed, we know all too well that in most cases—if not in every case—God will not heed our prayer. We all still die. The kingdom has not yet come. Still, if what I have been saying about prayer is anywhere near the truth, this silence and absence of God is not the end but precisely the beginning of prayer. Prayer is not a technique for getting what we want (if so, we would do well to discard it). It is calling out to the one who is absent to come near, to be present, to be as he has promised.

At this point we ministers and priests may seek refuge in our pastoral responsibility. Isn't it our duty to help another to trust God? And if we expose this other to God's absence, God's silence, will we not then destroy that trust? This example illustrates how frighteningly easy it is to justify illusion by an appeal to faith. Is it then any wonder that superstition takes the place of faith, and the world suspects that faith is simply illusion? We have brought this consequence on ourselves. In seeking to defend the faith, we have brought it into disrepute. We still do not believe that the truth will make us free (John 8:32)—we still fear that it will destroy us.

Pastors and priests must frequently face a further difficulty: that people pray for the healing they need, and become angry with God when they do not receive it. At this point our natural

reaction is to make excuses for God, to explain his ways. I
have already said that this is inappropriate because it is beyond
our competence. How much better it would be if we simply
helped our friend to express that anger—to God. After all,
it is not we who must give an accounting, as the story of Job
illustrates. Job wanted God to explain the reason for his circumstances, but his "friends" wished to give him explanations. The problem is not so much that their explanations
were false, but that they were *their* explanations, which only
left Job alone and unanswered. In the story God himself gave
an answer. And the point of the story is not, I think, that
God's explanation was *the* right and satisfying answer, but
that it was *God's* answer. Properly speaking, God could have
given the answer attributed to any one of Job's friends, but so
long as they were making excuses for him, there was no room
for God to speak.

We pastors and priests do similar damage in our usual response to pain and to the anger that follows from "unanswered" prayer. Our excuses serve to deflect the supplicant
from God and to insure that God will be silent, that his response will not be heard. With such excuses we offer a monologue in place of prayer. Shall we offer our stones to one
who asks for God's bread? Do we really imagine that our
explanations will satisfy the petitioner's hunger for God? And
if we succeed in this unholy transubstantiation (God forbid),
what then becomes of faith and prayer?

However painful, our responsibility to our neighbor is to
offer his or her need to God. Our intercessory task is to
dare to address that agony to the one who is our common Lord.
This is so even if it means that we pray the prayer of our
common Mediator: "My God, my God, why hast thou forsaken me?" Only then may we truly begin to bear one another's burdens, thus fulfilling the law of the one who has
borne all our burdens.

CHAPTER THREE
Prayer as Formation

What does prayer mean for the character of our life, for the shape of our existence? That Christian existence is founded upon and formed by prayer is scarcely a novel observation. It is one that can be read in many books and heard in many sermons. We may even hear that Christian existence *is* prayer, an assertion I also believe to be true. But in addition it is, as ordinarily understood, a gross distortion both of Christian existence and of prayer. In this chapter I want to reflect on one of the most curious assertions about prayer to be found in the New Testament: Paul's injunction to "pray without ceasing" (Rom. 12:12; I Thess. 5:17; Eph. 6:18). How is this injunction to be understood? Is it possible to make any sense of it in and for our daily lives in the world?

A. PRAY WITHOUT CEASING

Many people believe that what is involved here is a quantitative assertion about prayer—namely, that we ought to pray more often. Accordingly, people sometimes discipline themselves to pray more frequently and for increasingly lengthy periods. Or, more likely, people assume that Paul's command may be applicable to some—namely, to those worthy individuals who have a special "vocation" for prayer—but most certainly not to all Christians equally. These interpretations of Paul's command involve very real dangers. The first is that in increasing the times we pray, we simply increase our tendencies toward pseudo-prayer. In the preceding chapters we have explored numerous ways in which our prayer may be false, thus producing practical atheism, superstition, and idolatry. A great many of the books and "aids to prayer" that aim at "improving our prayer life" succeed only in destroying honest prayer. Added to this is the danger that we will simply absolve ourselves from attempting to understand the meaning of this commandment by claiming that it applies only to "someone else."

How, then, are we to understand this injunction, to avoid misapplying it in our practice of prayer? Is this an additional and impossible law in the face of which we have to admit our guilt and inadequacy? Or is it a word of help that illumines and makes sense of our life?

Let me indicate from the outset that I am not at all interested in persuading people to pray more often than they currently do. I know, of course, that there is supposed to be a crisis associated with prayer—that more and more people seem to find themselves praying less and less. But I am by no means persuaded that this is a bad thing. If we are gradually weaning ourselves from magical, idolatrous, and superstitious kinds of prayer, that can only be good. My concern is not that people pray more often, but that they pray more boldly, more truthfully, more clearly. This is the reason that I am directing attention primarily to those occasions on which we normally pray—in the gathered worship of our community of faith. That we are to pray without ceasing is not to be understood as a new law to be grudgingly obeyed or to be deceitfully avoided.

But if this is so, then how are we to respond to Paul's injunction? We should first notice that Paul's advice to "pray without ceasing" does not involve a quantification of prayer. He does not ask his churches to "pray more often" or "more regularly" or "for more hours" but "without ceasing." Paul knows perfectly well that people have much to do, much that cannot be done with eyes closed and hands folded, as even the most cursory glance through his letters makes clear. No multiplication of petitions add up to "without ceasing"—and, furthermore, the usual advice about setting aside regular blocks of time for prayer is a most unthinkable practice for the apostle who berated his congregation for "observing times, seasons . . ." (Gal. 4:10). This is not to deny that many people may find it helpful to pray at regular times during the day, while others may find this practice entirely arbitrary and most unhelpful. I have no advice to give about this matter, except to say that it has nothing whatever to do with the meaning of prayer or the injunction to pray without ceasing.

Help in understanding this injunction comes from relating it to another of Paul's seemingly odd pieces of advice: "Present your bodies as a reasonable worship" (Rom. 12:1). This advice is clearly related to the injunction to pray without ceasing, because it is repeated almost immediately in almost the same form in the letter to the Christians in Rome: "Be constant in prayer" (Rom. 12:12).

What is meant by presenting our bodies as a "reasonable" (i.e., rational, intelligent, conscious—literally, "logical") worship? The meaning of this passage remains obscure unless we understand that Paul usually uses the word "body" to indicate our relationship to others and to the world. He may understand this as a body of sin and death, as a "body of glory" (I Cor. 15), or, in this passage, as a body "holy and acceptable to God." The point here is that "body" refers to all our ways of relating to one another and our world (Käsemann). The term does not designate an object, and certainly not a "biological object," but a complex and intricate set of relationships. "Body" designates the form of our life in the world. Far from indicating some strange new law, an especially odd and extreme injunction, Paul's advice to "present your bodies as an intelligent worship" is the very foundation for all ethical pronouncements (Käsemann).[1]

If we place the injunction to "pray without ceasing" or "persist in prayer" in this context, then we see that what is involved here is our whole lifestyle. To pray without ceasing does not mean to engage in a particular sort of religious activity, but to shape all of our life in a particular way, to give our life in the world the structure of prayer. *To persist in prayer means that what we pray determines how we live.*[2]

[1] Ernst Käsemann, "Worship in Everyday Life: A Note on Rom. 12" in *New Testament Questions of Today*, Eng. tr. (Fortress, 1969), pp. 188-195. Moltmann takes this a step further when he claims that "worship has priority over ethics" (*The Church in the Power of the Spirit*, p. 271).

[2] This insight has been approximated by several of the theologians who in the history of the church have sought to understand the character of prayer. Echoing the connection between loving God and caring for one's brother (and sister), made so rigorously in I John 4:14f., Cyprian observes

Here we have, then, the basis for an understanding of prayer as the formation of life. Prayer is the mold in which the character of our life is shaped. It is when our existence is shaped by the longing that dares to hold God to his promise, to call him "Father," and to pray "your kingdom come" that we "pray without ceasing."

Thus prayer is not to be understood as one activity among others, as a time set apart from our daily and worldly life. It is not an exercise that disconnects us from our relationships with each other and our world so that we can "be alone with God." So complete is our confusion at this point that we

---

that ". . . if we call God father we ought to act as his children" (*On the Lord's Prayer*, 11 [p. 450]), and Origen notes that to pray without ceasing means "to combine with prayer the needful deeds and the prayer with the fitting actions." It is then that we can understand Christian life "as one great unbroken prayer of which prayer that is commonly called prayer is a part" (*On Prayer*, XII, 2 [p. 262]).

It is Aquinas, however, who, with characteristic precision and clarity, articulates the principle most fundamentally: "Length of prayer consists not in praying for many things, but in the affection persisting in the desire of one thing" (*Summa Theologica*, II, II, Q. 83, Art. 14, p. 1549). This is admirably exact. That it is said by one whose own life was organized by the succession of set-aside hours for prayers and by the disciplines of meditation and contemplation is all the more remarkable. Continuous prayer, he is saying, does not require these things at all (though he does make room for them, almost as an after-thought), but consists of the persistent desire for one thing. What is that one thing? Aquinas knows perfectly well: "Thy kingdom come." This simple desire expresses itself quite directly in a life of love, for—and here he quotes Augustine—"faith, hope and charity are *by themselves* a prayer of continual longing" (*Ibid*; cf. Augustine, *Letter CXXX*, xiv, 19 [p. 465]). Thus, for Aquinas, prayer is continuous "by reason of its effect whether in the person who prays . . . or in some other person . . ." (p. 1549).

Karl Barth's intention to use a commentary on the Lord's Prayer as the basis for a discussion of Christian ethics (*Church Dogmatics*, IV/4 [fragment], p. ix), though never completed, is the suggestion that has most stimulated my own reflections in this chapter. (Note: It was after I completed my book that Eerdmans published, in 1981, Karl Barth's *The Christian Life*, translated by Geoffrey W. Bromiley. While I still find Barth's use of the category of command inappropriate in connection with prayer, his reflections on the first three petitions of the Lord's Prayer are of great importance to anyone who seeks to understand prayer or the Christian life.)

I am also indebted to Don Saliers' excellent article "Prayer and Lifestyle." Saliers' thesis is that "in corporate worship, Christians engage in activities which articulate and shape how they are to be disposed toward the world" (p. 56). To this may be added Ebeling's remark that, "rightly understood, prayer is in a certain sense life in its most concentrated form" (*On Prayer*, p. 139; cf. p. 40).

would do well to say that prayer is not a religious or pious act at all. It is instead the form of our worldly, bodily, and daily activities. Continuous prayer means the whole of our life—not primarily our life alone but our life in community, not our life in "the church" but our life in the world, not our "devotional life" but our active life, not our "religious life" as such but our economic, political, and sexual life.

But let us not misunderstand. To say that prayer is the form of our everyday life is not to say that we should quit praying and get on with living. Honest, bold, and truthful prayer is not opposed to life in the world, nor is it a matter of alternatives—"work or pray." As most of us know, we are exhorted to work *and* pray. Of course, much of what passes for prayer is so utterly unworldly, unrealistic, dishonest, and superstitious that it truly does stand in fatal contrast to meaningful involvement in the fullness of life. Even worse, this sort of prayer may function simply as a respite from worldly life, leaving the alienating structures of work and action unchanged. Times of prayer then become temporary and refreshing escapes from the old earth to the old heaven—rather than the plea for "a new heaven and a new earth," for the rule of God on earth as in heaven.

But all of this has nothing to do with the prayer we have been describing as prayer "in Jesus' name." This prayer is neither an escape from worldly life nor an alternative to involving ourselves in the life of our neighbor. Prayer "in Jesus' name" is prayer that forms our life in the world. Without that form, our life is chaotic, fragmented, and riddled with the false, alienating anxieties and needs that are the very lifeblood of a world based on consumption and filled with distractions. Prayer is the articulation of that "one desire" that seeks not the perpetuation of the status quo but the transformation of all creation.

The activity of praying, then, is the activity of shaping and forming a style of life, a way of being in the world (though not determined by the world, and therefore not of the world). All along I have pointed to the liabilities of careless, thoughtless, and faithless prayer, and we see now why these liabilities are so serious. Prayer is not a matter of an occasional pious phrase, of an hour here or there; prayer is life-forming. Shapeless prayer produces chaotic life vulnerable to whatever in the world exerts the greatest force. False and superstitious prayer forms false and superstitious lives. For this reason, properly understanding prayer should not be the exclusive concern of specialists, whether they be liturgists or theologians. It is a matter of grave consequence for all Christians.

If, then, prayer forms our life, what kind of life is shaped like prayer "in Jesus' name"? This is not a matter that can be left out of a consideration of true prayer, but it is also a matter that is too extensive (covering, as it must, the whole character of Christian life) to be thoroughly treated in a book of this size and scope. My compromise will be to explain briefly some of the features of existence that most obviously correspond to the character of our prayer. In this way we can compose a brief sketch of our lives insofar as they are determined by the "desire for one thing" (Aquinas) for which we pray "in Jesus' name."

B. WITH OPEN EYES: ABIDING IN THE TRUTH

A life shaped like a prayer and formed by prayer—what is that like? Whatever else it is, *it is not a life lived with one's eyes closed! A life formed by prayer is a life opposed to illusion, self-deception, and hypocrisy.*[3] This needs to be said and heard again and again. In the face of every superstitious rationalization for prayer, against every superstitious defense of prayer, it must be said that prayer is at war with falsehood. Contrary to what the opponents of prayer—and, far more often, its "defenders"—frequently maintain, prayer is not and cannot be a refuge for wishful thinking. If one wishes to escape from reality, if one fears the truth, then one simply cannot pray, because prayer banishes illusion. Since it is our crying out in need— indeed, since it gives us practice in perceiving our need— prayer banishes the delusions of self-sufficiency in which we cloak ourselves and our world. In prayer we learn to see our-

---

[3]So important is this for Barth that he actually suggests that this is the reason for the command to pray: "In prayer—and this is why it is commanded—all masks and camouflages fall away" (*Church Dogmatics*, III/4, p. 98; cf. Ellul, *Prayer and Modern Man*, p. 1503).

selves and our world in the light of God's promise. It is this promise that exposes the pretended absolutes of our lives and opens our eyes to our own godlessness and godforsakenness.

Nothing is more incompatible with prayer than the rosy glow of piety with which we often seek to hide ourselves from one another or to justify the world's status quo. To avoid such delusions it is also important to expose and refute many of the ways in which prayer is defended and God is "excused" from "answering" prayer. Persistence in prayer, in the call for God to fulfill his promises—this persistence makes impossible all wishful thinking about the answering of prayer. If wishful thinking is banished here, it is banished everywhere. But it is important to realize that abolishing prayer in order to abolish illusion can be at least as productive of superstition as the pious and religious "defense" of prayer. On the basis of a supposed "critique of religion," some people dissociate wishful thinking from prayer—only to associate it with the state, the system, progress, the people, or "human potential." This Marxist, capitalist, or humanist "secularization" does not banish wishful thinking; it only encourages the proliferation of every form of wishful self-deception. A life shaped like prayer shuns this kind of wishful thinking, this illusion and self-deception.

Persistence in prayer, as Aquinas noted, "consists not in asking for many things but in . . . the desire of one thing."[4] This concentration upon "one thing" constitutes a fundamental focusing and centering of life, which breaks the spell of distraction. Confused by a world largely comprised of false needs and competing desires, we often say that we really do not know what we want. As consumers, citizens, and individuals, we are bewildered and distracted. Prayer is certainly no panacea for this pervasive confusion, but the concentration and focus concomitant to persistent prayer help to shape ways of living that strengthen our capacity to withstand distraction. Persistence in prayer helps us to know what we want. It is this knowledge alone that can help us withstand the temptation of the artificial needs and desires spawned by the world in which we live.

---

[4]*Summa Theologica*, II, II, Q. 83, Art. 14, p. 1549.

A centered and focused existence is a result of concentrating on "the desire of one thing." But it must be made clear that this thing is not an arbitrary and exclusive selection of one thing from among the many things we might need or desire. This one thing is that which prayer desires—nothing less than the kingdom of God, on earth as it is in heaven. It is therefore not a desire for heaven that opposes or excludes earth; the desire for the reign and rule of God "on earth as it is in heaven" excludes every form of dualism. The "one thing" desired by prayer is not an exclusive but a comprehensive thing: it includes the earth. Just as God's single promise is articulated in a variety of ways in the history of Israel and the Church, so also the one need for God includes our need for air and food, for justice, liberty, and love. These many needs are unified and ordered by the desire for the one thing that prayer desires—the coming of God, the transformation of heaven and earth. A life shaped like a prayer, a life formed by prayer is, then, a life that unites the fragments of our existence and centers itself in that one desire that both includes and orders all our needs.[5]

Karl Barth has characterized faith as "seeing clearly."[6] Prayer, as the yearning for God in the midst of our godforsakenness, is that which models and forms this clear vision, and the life formed by this prayer is one that "sees clearly." The frequently heard injunction to "watch and pray" makes clear the connection between prayer and "living with our eyes open." In the very different tradition of French mysticism, Simone Weil describes the character of Christian life as "attentive" existence.[7] It is this attentiveness and clarity that should characterize our existence, insofar as it is shaped like prayer "in Jesus' name." Of all the authors of the New Testament, none is as preoccupied with this dimension of Chris-

[5]So far as I can see, this is the only justification for Origen's claim that "he whose mind is set on prayer is in some sense profited merely by the settled condition involved in praying" (*On Prayer*, VIII, 2 [p. 255]). The danger is that this claim will become a reduction of prayer to self-therapy and auto-suggestion—a temptation to which Augustine in particular appears to be susceptible (*Letter CXXX*, ix [p. 465f.]).

[6]Karl Barth, *Romans*, Eng. tr. (Oxford, 1933), pp. 45ff.

[7]See Simone Weil, *On Science, Necessity, and the Love of God* (Oxford, 1968), pp. 148-159.

tian existence as is the author of the Gospel of John, who speaks of life as a "doing of the truth" (John 3:21) in the name of the one who is "the truth." Certainly no greater heresy exists in our churches and our theology than the refusal to accept and rejoice in the truth. Much theology, whether liberal or conservative, gives the impression that truth is feared. And much of church life and language suggests that we are evading the truth. All of this, whether liberal or conservative, can only be a betrayal of the character of faith.

In summary, a life shaped like prayer in Jesus' name will be a life which, at whatever cost, is an abiding in the truth, a doing of the truth, and will therefore be a life which is at war with every form of pious or secular self-deception, illusion, and wishful thinking. It is a dreadful irony that it is precisely in speaking about prayer that we seem most prone to self-deception, evasion, and rationalization. The resulting deformation of prayer can only result in a corresponding deformation of the lives of we who pray.

C. WITH OUR NEIGHBOR: SOLIDARITY WITH THE OTHER

What kind of living is shaped like prayer "in Jesus' name"? Whatever else it is, *it cannot be a life spent alone and apart from our neighbor. A life shaped like prayer is a life of openness to and solidarity with the neighbor.*

First of all, a prayer-like life is one of openness to the other. Most of us spend the majority of our time hiding behind our defenses, our pretenses. We pretend to be better than we are—wiser, stronger, more pious, more mature. We not only hide from one another—we hide from ourselves.

But in honest prayer we come to see ourselves as we are. We see our need, our lack, our yearning; we see ourselves in all our godlessness and godforsakenness. To the extent that prayer is honest, it discloses the secrets of our hearts, exposing to light the creeping fears and gaping void in the darkness of our minds.

But if in prayer we are exposed in both our large and petty deceptions, how can we attempt to rebuild these defenses and pretenses? If we are exposed to God, how can we hide from our sisters and brothers? It is not so much that we seek to live "without defenses," for this can become a new and altogether intrusive law; it is rather than pretense and posturing are no longer worth the effort. Who, after all, would we be trying to kid? If we cannot hide from God, what is the point of trying to hide from one another?

This, I believe, is the reason why Jesus found the religious posturing of the "righteous" so reprehensible, especially when this posturing took the form of an ostentatious display of prayer. In such prayer we find the opposite of true prayer, which shatters pretense. We also see its opposite in the incessant chatter about our "prayer life." Thus, apart from that prayer that cannot be dispensed with in the worship of the gathered community, it is best that prayer be "closeted," lest in making it public we use it to hide ourselves from one another, from ourselves, from God. Jesus' injunctions about praying in secret serve the interests of prayer that opens life—to God and to our neighbor.

A life shaped like a prayer is a life that is in fundamental solidarity with the neighbor. If pretense and posturing are eroded by prayer, then the divisions and discriminations that separate us from one another cannot stand. How can a discrimination between rich and poor survive the prayer in which we give expression to our need, pain, and brokenness? How can a discrimination between the good and the bad survive the prayer that grows out of our common godforsakenness? How can the distinction between the pious and the impious, the righteous and the unrighteous, survive the prayer that cries out for God in our common godlessness? The grace of God, which, as Paul says, "justified the ungodly" (Rom. 4:5), cannot possibly provide us a vantage point from which we are right while others are wrong. As Barth so truly says, "It is as and when we know that we are sinners that we know that we are brothers."[8] We may even learn to abandon the discrimination between brothers and sisters!

Thus the rule of life governed by prayer is that "nothing human is alien to me." I cannot separate myself from the needy, because I myself am needy. I cannot separate myself

[8]Barth, *Romans*, p. 101.

from the impious, because I myself am godless. I cannot separate myself from the sick, the handicapped, the aged, because I myself am a "being unto death" (Heidegger). Jesus depicts two kinds of prayer that characterize two styles of life: "Lord, I thank thee that I am not as others are" and "Lord, be merciful to me, a sinner." Existence shaped by the second prayer is life lived in unbroken solidarity with the neighbor—it is life lived even in solidarity with the pharisee!

D. WITH OUR HANDS: INVOLVEMENT IN PROTEST

What is the shape of a life that is a continuous prayer? Whatever else it is, *it is most decidedly not a life lived with folded hands. It is, instead, a life of active involvement in the needs of the neighbor, a life of protest against the godlessness and godforsakenness of our world.*

Unfortunately, it is possible to gain the impression that a life of prayer stands in contrast to a life of action and involvement. The notion that the one case has to do with God and religion while the other has to do with the world and politics has become so commonplace that we no longer notice its absurdity. This utter confusion then takes its revenge in the opposition of "conservative" and "liberal," of the personal and the social, of piety and activism.[9] In this way we seek to undo the Incarnation: to have God without the world, to have the world without God. In this way we set ourselves resolutely against God's election, action, and promise: against God's election and decision to "love the world"; against God's action in Christ's taking on our flesh to reconcile the world to himself; against God's promise of the transformation of earth into the "new creation." Nothing so clearly testifies to the apostasy of the church in our time as this renunciation of the Incarnation, and one of the clearest demonstrations of this apostasy is the opposition of prayer and involvement.

In prayer we pray with the whole community for the sake of the world. This is the essential character of prayer "in

[9]Moltmann argues forcefully against these oppositions; cf. *The Church in the Power of the Spirit*, pp. 282-288.

Jesus' name." In prayer we act in solidarity with our neighbor, a solidarity that has its basis in our hope for God's reign—a reign that comes not to one or two but to the earth. God's reign does not and cannot come for me apart from my neighbor. This would be the reign of some god other than the Father of Jesus who "so loved *the world* that he sent his only Son" (John 3:16; italics mine). If we have any hope, it is only insofar as there is hope for our neighbor. In prayer we enter into solidarity with our neighbor on the basis of our hope in God's promise—and on the basis of need. It is when we know what we need that we know that we are, in fact, sisters and brothers. In prayer, then, we give voice to our neighbor's need as our need. This solidarity, implicit in every word of our prayer (as soon as we call out "Our Father"), becomes explicit in the prayers of intercession.

I cannot pray for my neighbor if I am oblivious to my neighbor's real misery, yearning, and need. In intercession I identify with the actual pain and brokenness of my neighbor and our world in such a way that I call upon God to come, to address this pain and brokenness not only in general but in particular. In prayer my neighbor's misery becomes my own. If this is so, how may I then forget my neighbor's need, avoid my neighbor's misery, flee my neighbor's yearning? Is it really possible to honestly ask God to meet my neighbor's need and then act as if I am deaf to my neighbor's cry? Can I in fact so contradict with my life that for which I pray?

Here I must re-emphasize the point that the relationship between prayer and lifestyle is intrinsic to our prayer itself. In the Lord's Prayer we pray, "Forgive us our debts, as we also forgive our debtors." This petition takes three basic forms. In the Gospel of Matthew we find, "Forgive us our debts, as we have forgiven our debtors." In Luke we find, "Forgive us our sins, as we forgive our debtors." And in some versions of the English liturgy we have "Forgive us our trespasses, as we forgive those who trespass against us," or "Forgive us our debts, as we forgive our debtors." These variations of the petition are different in important ways. What is common to them all, however, is the explicit and direct connection between what we ask God to do and what we do. This connection is not an invention of Jesus; it is already a part of the Jewish tradition.[10] But Jesus gives it an unmistakable emphasis.

There must be no mistake. If I pray "in Jesus' name," I also ask God to deal with me as I deal with my neighbor, to release, liberate, and justify me *as* I also release, liberate, and justify my neighbor—a petition that should make us gasp in horror when we utter it. This is by no means an incidental feature of prayer. It is in fact the one petition that Jesus explicitly comments upon, as though to *underscore* the connection (Matt. 6:14).[11]

1. The Social Character of Prayer

If in fact our lives are in their very shape a continuous prayer, a persistent prayer, then *what do our lives ask for*? Do we ask God for justice or injustice? Do we ask him to meet our needs or to ignore them, to feed us or to let us starve, to set us free or to imprison us? What do we do? What do we not do? For what do we pray when our eyes are open and our hands are active?

If we are deaf to the cries of the hungry, the oppressed, the despised, and the needy, Jesus' word about the consequences is terrifying: "As you do . . . so shall it be done to you." And in our comfortable air-conditioned sanctuaries, in our well-fed sleepiness with our minds half-occupied by the Sunday roast in the oven, in our "Sunday best," in our oblivion and smugness, we pray—every Sunday—out loud: "Forgive us our debts, as we forgive our debtors." Have we gone utterly mad? If we do not intend to liberate the captive, feed the hungry, and open up the jails and "asylums," then let us by all

[10]*Ecclesiasticus* (The Wisdom of Jesus the Son of Sirach), circa 180 B.C.: "Forgive your neighbor the wrong he has done, and then your sins will be pardoned when you pray.

Does a man harbor anger against another and yet seek for healing from the Lord?

Does he have no mercy toward a man like himself and yet pray for his own sins?" 28:2-4

We must certainly reckon with the possibility that Jesus of Nazareth knew and applied this perspective of Jesus, son of Sirach. A difference is that this perspective is actually incorporated into the prayer itself.

[11]Thus Cyprian can argue that, given the force of this petition, we cannot expect to be forgiven if we are engaged in enmity with our neighbors (*On the Lord's Prayer*, 24 [p. 454]).

means quit praying. It's not just that we then have no right to pray—it is that it is insane to call down curses upon our own heads. Nor am I able to separate myself from the evidently fallen and misguided community in order to pray this prayer with an easier conscience, for I pray, "Forgive *us* as *we* forgive. . . ." This is quite different from asking God to deal with me as the best of us deal with our neighbors, a petition that is only another version of "I thank God I am not as others." I either pray with the community, however broken and hypocritical, or I do not pray at all—not, at least, "in Jesus' name." Forgetting this only makes a prophetic critique of the church into a pharisaic one.

There is, then, some urgency to the question, how are our lives shaped like a prayer? Moreover, it is only in facing this question that we can possibly ask whether our "prayers" have been answered.

As pointed out earlier, a life shaped like a prayer is one deeply involved in my neighbor's actual neediness. In identifying with my neighbor's need I can no more ignore any dimension of that need than I can ask for only a partial coming of God's reign, of his rule and presence. Still less can I separate my neighbor's "spiritual" need from his or her physical needs. To make this separation would be to revoke the central goal of our prayer—"as in heaven, *so on earth.*"

Thus I seek to meet my neighbor's actual need insofar as I act in conformity with my prayer. This means responding to the well-known imperatives: feeding the hungry, visiting the imprisoned and the sick, clothing the naked. By now it shouldn't be necessary to stress these self-evident applications of our prayer to our life.

But it is necessary to stress the way in which these actions must be placed in their actual economic, social, and political setting.[12] That our existence is bodily existence means that

[12]The earlier theologians do not often discuss the political character of prayer. However, Augustine does apply the phrase "Our Father" in the following way: "Here also there is an admonition to the rich and to those of noble birth, so far as this world is concerned, that when they have become Christians they should not comport themselves proudly towards the poor and the low of birth; since together with them they call God 'Our Father'— an expression which they cannot truly and piously use, unless they recognize that they themselves are brethren" (*Sermon on the Mount*, IV, 16 [p. 39]).

it is set within a network of relationships, as we have already seen. To deal with the bodily need of our neighbor is to deal with this system of relationships, these structures, which are the "principalities and powers" of our age and our world. Hunger is not "randomly distributed" across the globe; it is concentrated in the so-called "third world." Other injustices are similarly predictable: the poor die of diseases that the rich never even contract; blacks are imprisoned for crimes for which whites are not even prosecuted; programs of economic development regularly enrich the educated and turn the poor into impotent clients. In short, hunger, poverty, powerlessness, and sickness do not occur at random; they are structured by systems of political and economic privilege. If in our prayer we cry out against the need, the hunger, the poverty, and the powerlessness of our neighbor, we also cry out against and protest those structures and systems of relationship that enforce and organize our neighbor's need. If we do not do so, we simply acquiesce and collaborate in creating and perpetuating our neighbor's plight. To act in conformity with our prayer, therefore, is to protest political and economic structures of exploitation and deprivation.

This is all the more obvious if we once more reflect upon the character of that promise which is the source and goal of our prayer. That for which we hope is "the reign and rule of God," an alternative structure of relatedness that replaces injustice with justice, hunger with feasting, isolation with fellowship. We await not the destruction of the body but the resurrection of the body and, therefore, the transformation of a system of relatedness based upon death and greed into a system of interrelatedness expressive of life and love. It is this for which we pray when we pray, "Thy kingdom come." If our action is to conform to our prayer, it must expose this contradiction of worlds, of ages, of structures.

Separating prayer from politics results in the destruction of the prayer itself. A life shaped like a prayer will be one committed to economic and political liberation as it is also committed to other forms of liberation. Liberation theology is not one theology among others; true Christian existence is by definition involved in liberation.

2. The Necessity of Prayer

We have seen that engagement on the side of the needy, the oppressed, and the poor is essential to prayer—is, in fact, prayer as lifestyle. Some claim that this style of life is preferable to prayer and is a proper substitute for it, but such a claim, however well-intended, must be rejected. The call for unremitting activism on the side of the dispossessed can have no serious and fundamental basis apart from God's promise "to set at liberty those who are oppressed." And our involvement can have no real anchor apart from the persistent cry for that liberation, apart from the demand that God be who he has promised to be, which *is* our prayer. Apart from the clarity and seriousness that characterizes prayer "in Jesus' name," we could not clearly discern the magnitude of our own need or that of our neighbor. We would be endlessly tossed about by a bewildering succession of claims, needs, and desires were it not for the concentration and focus supplied by our prayer. Indeed, apart from this prayer it is by no means clear that we have neighbors at all (as distinct from allies and enemies, constituencies and class foes, etc.). It is precisely in and through our prayer that we gain the necessary solidarity and clarity to be engaged in our neighbor's protest against the godlessness and godforsakenness of our world. How, then, shall we abandon prayer in favor of involvement? How could such prayerless activism be "for our neighbor's sake"?

Of course the plea for such a prayerless activism often stems from the inactive and inert prayer of our communities. If it comes to a choice between these two impossibilities (for at bottom they are impossible), then there can be no doubt where we must stand. The words of Matthew 25 in the so-called "parable of the sheep and the goats" makes it unavoidably clear. The "judge" asks not "who called me Lord"—not even who confessed him as Lord, not even who proclaimed his lordship—but "who fed the hungry, clothed the naked. . . ." The last words—"Inasmuch as you did it for the least of these . . . you did it to me"—echo the words he has taught us to pray: "as we forgive our debtors." If we were to choose between a godless humanism and a misanthropic piety, we could not hesitate.

But such a choice is entirely artificial and arbitrary, one that seeks to divorce that which has been joined together "in Jesus' name," in his life and destiny. We cannot, for the sake of our neighbor, offer him our assistance *instead of* God's, our mercy *instead of* God's, our justice *instead of* God's. Can we cause the dead to live?

3. To Act is to Ask

It is this which brings us face to face with the basis, character, and goal of our action insofar as it is "on our neighbor's behalf" and "in Jesus' name." Our action on our neighbor's behalf by no means substitutes for God's action. It is instead an action that forms a prayer for God's action. The style of life that befriends the friendless asks God to befriend his world, and therefore us as well; the style of life that feeds the hungry asks God to "give us our daily bread"; the style of life that is governed by solidarity with the oppressed and the exploited asks God to bring his kingdom. To take seriously our neighbor's physical, economic, and political needs (not only her psychic or "spiritual" needs) is to ask that God accomplish his will "on earth as it is in heaven." *To act is to ask*.

It is also true that "to ask is to act." Prayer is above all action, a strenuous action that Ellul properly describes as combat. I do not think it is possible to take our neighbor's need with the seriousness which it deserves apart from this asking, petitioning, and interceding. Only in this way does the true dimension of our neighbor's plight become clear. And only in this way do we see that plight not as superficial or accidental or peripheral but as very real—and offensive. This is what it means to say that our lifestyle is a continuous prayer.

But our action is not "an answer to prayer"—it is the prayer itself. We know this most clearly when we have begun to fashion a lifestyle in which we take our neighbor's need as our own. In doing so we are confronted with the vastness of need and with the intractability of those "principalities and powers" that characterize our world's godlessness and godforsakenness. This is true no matter which dimension of our neighbor's need most concerns us. Who has searched out the depth of our neighbor's loneliness, the depth of his need for love and recognition? If we take the depth of this need and yearning with fundamental seriousness, do we not see an abyss of need? And who can count the number of our neighbors who have too little to eat, who die of starvation or are weakened by malnutrition? Who can solve the enormous complexities introduced into this picture by the competing claims of cultural autonomy, national independence, and systems of distribution? If we take seriously the extent and complexity of the task of feeding the hungry, do we not see a profound need? Equally complex is the task of freeing the oppressed—a task so immense that it can make us despair. If we add to this the dismal history of revolutions in the name of the oppressed that so regularly result in the creation of a new class of oppressors, a new set of "political prisoners," a new "reign of terror," how shall we find the courage to proceed?

Of course we could gain the courage to act by arbitrarily closing our eyes to the depth, the extent, the complexities of need—by claiming an absolute righteousness and effectiveness for our action. We could call to our aid the demons of "revolutionary necessity" or "national security," and categories such as "neurotic need" and "psychopathology." These no doubt have their place—but they become demonic when they serve only to obscure the true character of our neighbor's need. If, on the basis of the character of our prayer, we have put aside such wish-fulfilling and self-justifying veils of illusion, how shall we have the courage to act?

We can claim this courage precisely on the basis of God's promise. The basis for our action is the same as the basis for our prayer. It is precisely when we have seen the depth of our neighbor's need that we have reason to call for God's coming—to call for this both in word and deed. The immensity and complexity of our neighbor's need is no more a basis for not acting than it is a basis for not praying. The basis for our acting is not the illusion that we can meet our neighbor's need, but the hope that God will do so. We need have no silly illusions about "bringing in the kingdom." Just as the *shape* of our action is determined by the shape of our prayer, so the *basis* of our action is determined by the basis of our prayer, and the *goal* of our action is determined by the goal of our prayer. In our life in the world with our neighbor, we plead for God to come to us in our godlessness as he has promised: "on earth as it is in heaven."

A life shaped like a prayer is not a life lived with folded hands. It is one of involvement with our neighbor, of concrete aid to him or her. Thus it is also an involvement in protest against those economic, political, ideological, and psychological structures that are the guardians and enforcers of our godlessness. A life shaped like a prayer is a life of action that is without illusions about the ultimate efficacy of our action. *Like our prayer, our action is an asking for God.*

Existence shaped like a prayer in Jesus' name is not a life lived with eyes shut but an abiding in truth; not a solitary existence but a life lived in openness and solidarity with our neighbor; not a life of "folded hands" but a life of protest against the structures of oppression in our world. But whose life can claim to be thus shaped and formed? To make this claim about our lives is but to open the door again to the sham and pretense, the hypocrisy and self-deception that are the enemy of every true prayer. In this respect Paul also describes us when he says of himself: "The good that I would, I do not, and that which I would not do, I do" (Rom. 7:19). Far from constituting an unanswerable objection to prayer and to the shaping of life by prayer, however, this is but the return to the beginning. This is, for Paul as for us, not an objection to prayer but its basis: "Wretched man that I am, who will deliver me from this body of death?" (Rom. 7:24). We are returned to the origin of prayer in us: our godlessness and godforsakenness. It is because of this condition that we pray at all.

But what is involved here is not an orgy of self-flagellation, self-denunciation, and self-pity. Quite calmly and soberly we can admit of both our life and our prayer that "we cannot pray as we ought." But we may also say that in our incapacity the Spirit intercedes with us so that we can nevertheless say "Abba"—that is, we can pray, and therefore live. This capacity that intrudes upon our incapacity, this power that overwhelms our impotence, this life that invades our death speaks in and through us in a language both like and unlike that of prayer: the language of praise and thanksgiving.

PART II:
Praise and Thanksgiving in Jesus' Name

*I will give thanks to the Lord with my whole
    heart;*
  I will tell of all thy wonderful deeds.
I will be glad and exalt in thee,
  I will sing praise to thy name, O Most High.

·   ·   ·   ·   ·

The Lord is a stronghold for the oppressed,
  a stronghold in times of trouble.
*And those who know thy name put their trust in
    thee,*
  *for thou, O Lord, hast not forsaken those who
    seek thee.*

Sing praises to the Lord, who dwells in Zion!
  Tell among the peoples his deeds!
For he who avenges blood is mindful of them;
  he does not forget the cry of the afflicted.

·   ·   ·   ·   ·

For the needy shall not always be forgotten,
  *and the hope of the poor shall not perish
    for ever.*

Psalm 9:1-2, 9-12, 18

Our worship consists not only of prayer but of praise and thanksgiving as well. So closely bound together are praise and prayer that we often use the term "prayer" to describe them both. Though this usage tends to obscure the very great differences between these two actions, it does rightly suggest that no understanding of prayer is possible apart from a consideration of praise and thanksgiving. In the gathered Christian community, the words of prayer and the songs of praise serve as the alternating rhythm of our common worship. So fundamental are these actions that we may alternately describe our common worship as a "prayer service" (common prayer) or a service of praise and thanksgiving ("worship," "eucharist," "celebration"). In each case we describe the whole from the standpoint of a part. But it is not that our common prayer/worship consists of two parts that stand alongside one another or are arbitrarily alternated. These "parts" mutually interpret one another and presuppose one another. Prayer expresses our need and desire for God, a need that grows out of our godlessness and godforsakenness. Praise, on the other hand, grows out of the presence and self-giving of God, and therefore expresses our fullness and joy.

No simple hymn of praise can serve as the basis of our discussion here in the way in which the texts of the Lord's Prayer served our previous discussion. Moreover, we do not find in the history of theology any clearly developed treatises devoted to our present subject. This is due not to the lesser importance of praise but to its more self-evident character. The aim of our discussion is limited to exploring both the contrast between and the unity of prayer and praise, and to showing that this element of our common worship also has implications for our styles of living in the world. Accordingly, this discussion will be much briefer than our discussion of prayer. As with prayer, we will have to explore some of the potential abuses and misunderstandings associated with praise and thanksgiving, but these appear to be fewer in number and, for the most part, less serious than those associated with prayer. This may be due to the greater spontaneity and clarity of gratitude, unlike the bewilderment and confusion resulting from the need and lack that constitute our grounds for prayer.

We shall, however, continue to refer to the texts of the Lord's Prayer in order to determine what we have received. For it is in receiving that for which we pray that praise and thanksgiving have their basis and reason for being.

Here again we shall have to ask, what is the basic character of praise and thanksgiving? What are the chief types of praise? How does a life governed by praise take shape? In what way is our everyday existence a continuous song of praise? Praise is the "other side" of prayer; indeed, without praise, as we shall see, it is impossible to pray.

It is difficult to discuss praise and thanksgiving both clearly and critically. This is true not only because of the difficulty involved in talking about talking. This alone is difficult enough, because we have here no vantage point outside of language from which to view it "at a distance"; we are unable to get outside our linguistic skins. Speaking about praise is, of course, also difficult because it means making the transition from "speaking to" to "speaking about." It is like making the transition from talking with someone (a friend or lover, for example) to talking about what one has said or will say to that same one. These problems are difficult enough, but they are the same problems we encountered in talking about prayer.

However, in a discussion of praise and thanksgiving we encounter a further difficulty: the well-known one of describing joy, gladness, happiness. We all know that descriptions of trouble and calamity are always easier to attend to than descriptions of happiness. This is true in literature: it is easier, for example, to read and "enjoy" Dante's *Inferno* than his *Paradiso*, easier to appreciate Milton's *Paradise Lost* than his *Paradise Regained*. On a very different level, our newspapers also find it easier to pay attention to the "bad news" instead of the "good news"—and so do we, their readership. We quickly become bored by discussions of good, wholesome, and troublefree parts of life. This may be rooted in the character of language itself: perhaps our language is best at dealing with that which is absent. When we are full, for example, we don't talk much about food. The positive is simply "there"; there's not much to discuss. On the other hand, the negative generates a great deal of language, and quite interesting language at that. This explanation may also help account for a previously mentioned fact: that in the history of theology a number of treatises have been written on prayer, but very few have focused on praise and thanksgiving. Nevertheless, there are issues requiring clarification and misunderstandings needing correction if our praise and thanksgiving is to be honest and joyful.

CHAPTER FOUR
The Shape of Praise

Although the language of praise and thanksgiving is almost infinitely varied, it nevertheless exhibits constant and invariable characteristics so long as it is offered "for Jesus' sake." Accordingly, we must attempt to clarify these constant basic features before discussing the main varieties of this doxological language in our liturgy.

This discussion will rely upon the preceding discussion of prayer. Many of the elements of prayer also figure in praise, but these now have a different content and meaning. Because this difference determines the order in which we discuss these elements, the outline of this discussion is both like and unlike the outline of our discussion of prayer.

A. THE SPIRIT OF GOD

The origin of praise is the leaping of the Spirit within us, the outpouring of God's Spirit upon us. Just as prayer originates in the sighings and groanings of the Spirit, so praise is grounded in the "rush" of God's Spirit. Praise and thanksgiving is the way the Spirit's presence and power is articulated among us.

Talk of the Spirit is subject to two kinds of misunderstanding that must be particularly guarded against. The first is a "religious" or "pious" misunderstanding. Talk of God's Spirit quickly becomes talk of an "otherworldly" and "spooky" agency that evokes the claims of supernaturalism, spiritualism, and an unworldly "spirituality." Our language about the "gift of the Spirit" often takes on a specifically and narrowly religious meaning that strictly segregates the spiritual from the bodily and worldly. In strongest possible contrast to this is the biblical language about God's Spirit. In the Old Testament the term for Spirit is taken from the word for wind or gale. When this "wind of God" comes upon his creatures, they "come alive," become dynamic, energized, and active. It is the outpouring of the Spirit that causes the young to run, the lame to walk, the old to see. The overriding metaphor here is one of power that energizes God's creatures.

In English the best equivalent of this notion is our reference to a "spirited horse," or our saying, "She (or he) has real spirit" or referring to "team spirit."[1] Similarly, when one is downcast, despairing, without power or hope, we may say that he/she is "dispirited"—that is, without or deprived of spirit. This everyday usage of "spirit" is far closer to the biblical notion of Spirit than the religious usage, which inevitably gets associated with the half-alive, the unworldly, the non-bodily, and the narrowly pious. God's Spirit is that which gives life and makes it "lively." Nothing could be further from superstitious talk of the "spirits" of the dead. Though such a reference completely contradicts Hebrew thought, this is precisely the sort of metaphor that seems to govern most talk of "spirituality," "the spiritual life," and "gifts of the Spirit." This religious misunderstanding is so pervasive that it is almost impossible to speak meaningfully of the Spirit in anything like a biblical manner.

The second misunderstanding takes both pious and secular forms. It is the use of the notion of "Spirit" to designate something that is intrinsic to our being—some special capacity or dimension of our own existence. Although there is some biblical warrant for this notion, it is, in its main features, untenable. The Spirit is not "our spirit" but God's Spirit, which comes upon us from outside to make us alive and lively. The Spirit is God himself present in power to his creation. In the proper sense, then, we do not have "spirits"; God alone *is* Spirit (John 4:24).

Thus the theological meaning of "Spirit" stands equally opposed to "religious" and "secular," to pious and psychological uses of the term. To speak of Spirit is to speak of the

---

[1] I have found Pannenberg's discussion of the Spirit helpful (*The Apostle's Creed in the Light of Today's Questions*, Eng. tr. [Westminster, 1972]).

presence of the one who created heaven and earth for these creatures in such a way that he made them alive and therefore "spirited." It is in this "spirit" that we utter exclamations of praise and songs of thanksgiving, just as, in the same way, we may express being so "spirited" by running for the sheer joy of running.

We may gain additional clarity about the relationship of praise to the Spirit's presence if we remember that the Spirit is the presence "in advance" and in us of what God has promised. That God's Spirit "will be poured out on all flesh" is the way in which the prophet Joel speaks of the fulfillment of God's promise and his reign (Joel 2:28). Jesus begins his own ministry and mission with the text from Isaiah: "The Spirit of the Lord is upon me" (Luke 4:18; Isa. 61:1, 2). God's promise, then, is fulfilled in the Spirit's presence, a presence that is discerned when the blind see or the lame walk or the prisoners are set free or the hungry are fed or justice is done. It is then that we may speak of God's reign coming ahead of time, or of an "advance payment" of that which God has promised.

Moreover, the Spirit is the one through whom this occurs in us, not ahead of us (in the future) or above us (in "heaven"). To speak of God's Spirit is to speak not of the transcendence but the immanence of God; to speak not of God above or beyond us but in and through us. To say that God's Spirit is the origin of praise and thanksgiving, then, is to say that praise has its basis in the enlivening presence, in us, of that which God has promised.

B. THE PRESENCE OF GOD

The radical difference between prayer and praise is most evident in the difference between the ways these two activities characterize our existence. Prayer characterizes our life as needy and desiring, as godless and godforsaken; praise characterizes our life as full and joyous, as enlivened by the Spirit. Prayer expresses God's absence from us; praise expresses God's presence in us.

Much of our existence is characterized by unsatisfied needs, by unanswered desire. Much of the time we are afflicted by the sense that there is "not enough." Even when we surround ourselves with reasonable comfort (and even unreasonable luxury), we are still troubled by the anxiety that there is "not enough." Our existence, then, is characterized by the anxious quest for enough food, enough security, enough love, enough meaning—a drive that is self-defeating, because there is never "enough." Both capitalist and Marxist economic structures seek to enforce methods of distribution that make resources seem scarce. Both democratic and totalitarian political structures seek to ration the distribution of power and influence as "scarce goods." This scarcity produces necessity, because we are bound by our need for what we perceive as scarce. After all, life itself is scarce; existence is a degenerative disease.

In contrast is the sense that there is "more than enough." Life, instead of being scarce, is abundant. Nature seems not stingy but profligate. Or our loneliness is swept away by love and affection, our poverty by wealth. This experience may have the same objective "data" as that of poverty: the smile to which we were oblivious yesterday may be more than enough today, but not enough tomorrow. Abundance is not quantitative, not a matter of piling up sufficient quantities of what we need until at some point this amassing of goods tips the scales at "more than enough." It is not a matter of satiation, which produces only a temporary reprieve from necessity. That is not "more than enough" but only "enough for now."

Two words properly name the experience of "more than enough"—joy and gratitude. Gratitude is not a grudging acknowledgment of that which is "not enough" or "only enough": it is our response when we feel we have received more than enough. The word "gratitude" thus corresponds to "grace," which is the giving of more than we deserve or need. In fact, strictly speaking, we are not talking of two different things here, because gratitude is the name for what we feel when we experience grace. I am *grate-ful* when I am *filled* by the gracious excess and overflow and abundance of grace. This is quite different from the attempt to evoke or instill in someone a proper "gratitude"—an impossible task, because gratitude, like joy, is a feeling that cannot be coerced. It is the spontaneous, automatic response to "more than enough."[2]

Because the idea of gratitude is so spoiled for us by our attempts to coerce one another to be polite or to stop demanding more, the word "joy" may be more evocative for us as a way of naming the experience of "more than enough." When in the midst of our habitual anxiety we are overtaken and flooded with an excess and superfluity of life—this is joy. When joy is expressed in words or actions, we rightly call this "rejoicing."

"The fruit of the Spirit is . . . joy," writes Paul (Gal. 5:22). The joy that we feel whenever we sense that this smile, this food, this embrace, this insight is more than enough—this joy is the fruit of the Spirit. It is the hidden or manifest presence of that which is promised.

In discussing prayer I maintained that there was no pious or religious presupposition for prayer—only the sense of great need and yearning. A similar assertion can be made about praise and thanksgiving. When life is filled with liveliness, we feel joy and gratitude—feelings that we express in praise and thanksgiving.

C. THE ACTION OF GOD

Insofar as praise has its origin "in us" it is grounded in the sense of joy and gratitude that corresponds to the experience of "more than enough." But this is not the only basis for praise. Just as prayer has its basis in God's promise, and is therefore a claiming of that promise, so praise has its basis in God's action, and is therefore a celebration of that action and presence. In prayer we ask that God *will come* to us; in praise we rejoice that God *has come* to us.

What it means to say that God has come to us is clear when we review those petitions in which we call upon God to come to us. To say that God has come to us is to say that his name

[2]Barth's use of "gladly" (*gerne*) is an attempt to bring this to expression (*Church Dogmatics*, III/2, pp. 265-285). Paul's phrase in reference to grace— "how much more"—similarly stresses this "more than enough" (Rom. 5:10, 17, 20; I Cor. 6:3).

has been made holy, that his kingdom has come and that his end has been accomplished. It is to say that we have been fed and forgiven, that we have been delivered from evil. All of this is asserted and claimed on account of the life and death and resurrection of Jesus of Nazareth, who is the "Yes" to all God's promises because he is the presence of God in person. In him God not only has promised himself to us but has come to us. This is the meaning of the assertion that Jesus is the Christ of God, the Son of God, the Lord. It is through him that all claims to God's presence must receive their validation. This is the claim of Christian faith.

It is in the history and destiny of Jesus that God's name is hallowed. In Jesus, God is manifest as redeeming love and acquires the name Abba, meaning "Father." It is in and through Jesus that God comes to us as Father and thus "hallows his name." That Jesus is the manifestation of God is expressed most boldly by the words of the Gospel of John, in which Jesus is characterized as asserting "I and the Father are one" (John 10:30), and "He who has seen me has seen the Father" (John 14:9). Calvin explains this connection as follows: ". . . in calling God 'Father,' we put forward the name 'Christ.' With what confidence would one [otherwise] address God as 'Father'?"[3] That God's name is hallowed in Jesus is the central meaning of the claim that Jesus "reveals" or discloses God. This is not a matter of putting forward a series of propositions about the nature or character or will of God; it is the claim that we know God to be "Father" because and insofar as we know Jesus.

In the history and destiny of Jesus the reign and rule of God enters our world and our history. It is because and insofar as this is true that the Christian community already proclaims Jesus as Lord. The Lordship of Jesus is demonstrated in his authority, both his authority in matters of the Law shown in the Sermon on the Mount), and his sovereignty over the "demons" of sickness and madness which he exorcized. In these and a host of other ways the writers of the Gospels attest to

---

[3]*Institutes*, III, xx, 29, p. 892. Cf. also Ebeling's remark on the first petition that "God's becoming God takes place as God's becoming man" (*On Prayer*, p. 59).

the community's experience with and memory of Jesus as the one in and through whom God's reign has come upon us.

In the history and destiny of Jesus the will of God has been accomplished. It is because and insofar as this is true that Jesus is confessed as the one through whom humanity and the world are reconciled to God. It is in and through Jesus that the age-old enmity between ourselves and God (and therefore our enmity toward one another) is overcome and replaced with friendship.

Beyond this we may say that in the history and destiny of Jesus we have received our daily bread. Not only in the "feeding of the five thousand" but also in the stories of healing and help so frequent in the Gospels, Jesus is portrayed as one through whom the concrete needs of our neighbor are met—and not only met. The Gospel of John portrays Jesus beginning his ministry by transforming water into wine (John 2:1-11), an action in which need is met not with "enough" but with "more than enough."

In the history and destiny of Jesus "our sins are forgiven." Because and insofar as this is true, the Christian community confesses Jesus as Savior. In and through his freedom we are set free (Gal. 5:1).

Finally, in the history and destiny of Jesus we are delivered from Evil. It is because and insofar as this is true that the Christian community celebrates Jesus' Resurrection as the beginning and guarantee that the "last enemy" is overthrown (I Cor. 15). Therefore Jesus is called "the Christ," the liberator and redeemer of humanity.

The Christian community identifies Jesus as the one in whom God's promises are already fulfilled. But this "already" never becomes self-satisfied and backward-looking. Praise has not yet eliminated prayer—we still await and expect God's coming, which is "not yet" accomplished. Still, the basis of this waiting and hoping is that which has already been accomplished in Jesus. Thus praise is already possible because the one for whom we hope has already come.

The external and objective basis of praise and thanksgiving is God's action in the history and destiny of Jesus. It is this which properly founds and forms that gratitude and joy that is the internal, subjective basis for praise and thanksgiving.

The objective basis of praise (God's action) comes to us in the Spirit, whose presence and power creates the subjective basis of praise (gratitude and joy). Thus praise and thanksgiving do not originate in the work or power of just any spirit but the Spirit of Christ. It is this which makes impossible any random or arbitrary "spiritualism" or "spirituality," which prevents us from confusing the enlivening of the Spirit with the debilitating ravages of "spiritualistic" fever. If the Spirit by which we live and are enlivened is not "of Christ," then it will not produce true praise and thanksgiving. On the other hand, this connection between Jesus and the Spirit that makes us alive and lively makes it clear that no appeal to Jesus can legitimate a dead and deadly conformity, a passive and half-alive piety, a desperate and teeth-gritting obedience. For Jesus promises and bestows not religion but the Spirit, and the Spirit is not one of confusion or anonymity but the Spirit of Christ.

Since we are dealing with the praise and thanksgiving of the community, we may and must say that it has its actual and objective basis in God's action in the history and destiny of Jesus. It is this which determines that it is truly God's Spirit with us and in us that makes us alive and lively, and therefore grateful and joyful. Unquestionably, people experience joy and gratitude apart from any knowledge or reliance upon God's action in Jesus. Where this is so we may also suppose that God's Spirit is at work making these individuals alive and lively, so long as this liveliness occurs in ways compatible with the history and destiny of Jesus, which is the basis and test of the Spirit's activity. We will return later to this theme of the universality of the work of the Spirit, and therefore to the representative character of Christian praise and thanksgiving.

D. GRATITUDE FOR GOD

We give praise and thanksgiving not for many things but for one thing. In the expression of praise and thanksgiving we are not engaged in listing a miscellaneous and heterogeneous series of so-called "blessings." Just as it is a degradation and deformation of prayer to turn it into a shopping list addressed to a cosmic Santa Claus, so it is a degradation of thanksgiving to turn it into the avaricious game of counting the presents under life's Christmas tree. We give thanks not for many things but for one thing (so also we are enjoined not to give thanks *for some* things but *in all* things). We give thanks not for many blessings but for one blessing: that God is God, that God is Emmanuel—"God with us."

Failure to understand this basic principle of praise and thanksgiving produces obscene deformities in our language and our life. How often do we say, when we see some particularly unfortunate soul, "God has been good to me!" Far from being an expression of faith, this is an obscenity. To use the miseries of others as an incentive to "count our blessings" is an unmitigated blasphemy that turns God into a cosmic tooth fairy or the tribal deity of a fortunate "class." This grotesque distortion makes God a monstrosity, a capricious "dame fortune." Beyond this it substitutes greed for gratitude and pride for joy. Our joys are greatly diminished, not increased, by the miseries of others. Do we need to be reminded once again of the prayer of the pharisee: "I thank God I am not as others are . . ."? It is bad enough for this kind of praying to occur in private, or in a superstitious folk religion that worships fortune in the name of God. But that it should actually happen in the public liturgy and worship of Christians who pretend to be praying "in Jesus' name" is an outrage. The damage done here is incalculable, because it actually promotes a view of God and of life that is utterly antithetical to Christian faith. People who are regularly exposed to this sort of "thanksgiving" either will worship the false gods of fortune and caprice or, in rightly rejecting those demons, will reject the Christianity in whose name they have been enshrined.

It is heartbreaking to hear this sort of language from people whose motives may be presumed to be good, whose faith may be presumed to be genuine. They do so because they have "heard it in church." How long before the hearing and using of such language infects all gratitude with greed, infects faith with superstition? And when "misfortune" strikes, will these people not ask, with justice, what they have done to receive such a curse? Who is the God who inflicts such evil (did he not once give this and that "gift")? A host of misunderstand-

ings and "crises of faith" are produced by this horrifying confusion of God with fortune.

When we give thanks, we give thanks for God; when we
utter praise, we delight in God—God alone. True, we may
give thanks for many things for which we are grateful—but
grateful because we feel and know them to be signs of God's
love, of God's presence—that is, of God with us. It is only to
the extent to which this or that experience is known to be the
presence of the one who has promised himself to us that we
utter praise and thanksgiving.

We rejoice, then, in "one thing," not in "many things." But
this one thing is not merely one among others—it is, after all,
the presence of God, and therefore includes healing, liberation, and love. This is no random multiplicity; it is an ordered
plenitude, the fullness of God's rule and reign, his presence
and power.

The single focus or aim of our praise means that praise
may be characterized as a rejoicing in God, as an enjoyment
of or delight in God.

E. ADDRESS TO GOD

Like prayer, praise is directed to God. Thus we must distinguish praise and thanksgiving from a monologue in which we
remind ourselves to be grateful for this or that benefit, and
from a homily whereby we remind other poeple to be grateful
for their "blessings." These exercises may have a certain legitimacy and necessity, but they are not part of actual praise
and thanksgiving. They direct our attention to ourselves rather
than to God, to our feelings—our gratitude or ingratitude—
rather than to the gracious God who gives freely. It need
scarcely be added that praise and thanksgiving are to be distinguished from a directionless and amorphous feeling of being
pleased with ourselves or our world.

But we must again ask, to which God is our praise directed?
Are the words of our praise and thanksgiving those which
make it clear that we really know what has been given to us?
Or are these words betraying the fact that we have been so
inattentive and ungrateful that we have not even bothered to
"open the gift" or to know the giver? The very words we use

will indicate to whom our praise is directed: God the great candy machine, who gives us what we want, or God the Father, who gives us what we need; God the promoter, who helps us succeed, or the crucified God, who gives himself; God the genie, who fulfills our wishes, or the Creator of heaven and earth and Lord of history.

In the formulation or selection of hymns and liturgies of praise and thanksgiving, it is enormously important to be certain that the words we use do not make the praise and thanksgiving of the community into a meaningless and formless or superstitious and idolatrous exercise.

The form of praise and thanksgiving has a clearly trinitarian structure: praise is directed to God (the Father) on the basis of God's action (the Son), which is made present and enlivening by God's presence (the Spirit). This trinitarian structure is no empty or arcane theological abstraction; it provides us with practical, necessary guidance in formulating the praise and thanksgiving of the community. Because praise and thanksgiving is directed to God, it is distinguished from all formless, idiosyncratic, self-centered glee. Because it is founded upon the action of God, it is distinguished from all arbitrary and uncertain "counting of blessings." Because it is founded upon the presence of God, it is distinguished from all grudging and forced conformity to an external obligation or law.

F. COMMON PRAISE

Like prayer, praise is offered within the community. We may even say that it is impossible to praise and give thanks alone, because the song of praise requires the melody of many voices, the harmony of all creation. In this way praise corresponds to the one to whom it is offered—the creator of all. Our words and hymns of praise echo with this solidarity with all of creation.

The basis of our praise and thanksgiving is God's coming and the empowering, enlivening presence of the Spirit. But this Spirit is not the possession of an individual or a group; it is the Spirit of Christ, the Spirit which creates and recreates the earth, which is the gift given to all and for all. When and as we experience empowerment and enlivening, we experience in advance that Spirit which is to be poured out "on all flesh." The community is that historical reality which attests to the presence of this Spirit, and thus is the community of praise and thanksgiving. Similarly, praise and thanksgiving offered as the response to *this* Spirit must be communal and corporate. Otherwise the Spirit is demonic, bringing separation and isolation rather than the community of "all flesh."

From this point of view we can see why Paul is so adamant that any gift of the Spirit be related to the community—for the upbuilding of the community (I Cor. 12). For the benefit of the community Paul also insists that speaking in tongues must be accompanied by interpretation. The community is also the reason that the most important and most basic gift of the Spirit is, according to Paul, love (I Cor. 13). Clearly, a "spiriting" which drives us away from our sisters and brothers can only be demonic.

Thus praise as the response to the coming of this Spirit has its true place within the community. This is true even when we are physically alone, apart from our sisters and brothers, because the Spirit that enlivens us also unites us with the community. So it also is that the community, insofar as it is shaped by praise and thanksgiving, is united with "all the company of heaven."

In this discussion we have seen that praise, like prayer, is directed to God, is communal in character, and is based upon the work of God's Spirit. But, unlike prayer, praise is the expression of joy and fullness rather than godlessness and emptiness. It is grounded in the act rather than the promise of God, and is therefore related to the presence rather than the absence of God. The exact relationship between prayer and praise is one that we will define after we have investigated more closely the types of praise and the way in which praise shapes our existence.

CHAPTER FIVE

The Forms of Praise

Although the basic structure we have been considering applies to all acts of praise, praise does take various forms in the worship of the community. We will have to identify the most important kinds of praise in order to see how the concrete acts of praise exemplify this structure.

We will discuss four major varieties of "acts of praise." We will first consider "praise as adoration," which will include all of those liturgical forms that specifically focus on the character and being of God, among them being such familiar forms as the doxology and the Gloria Patri. The consideration of praise as adoration parallels the consideration of prayer as invocation. We will then discuss praise as thanksgiving, which is characterized by its enumeration of the variety of ways in which God comes to us. As such, the consideration of thanksgiving will parallel that of petition. Next we will consider rejoicing, making it clear that praise embraces not only our joy but our neighbor's joy as well, and so parallels the previous discussion of intercession. Finally, we will consider the offertory as one act of praise that is specifically inclusive of our bodily and worldly existence as enlivened by the Spirit.

This discussion is not a commentary on the texts of the various acts of praise. Such a commentary would necessarily focus on particular traditions within the one Church, and such a task would have to include a vast collection of materials ranging from traditional liturgical texts to the psalms to a large portion of the hymns of the various traditions and communities. Insofar as these are "acts of praise" they will reflect the features of the basic structure of praise, and of one or more of the types we will consider here.

The very diversity of the material that makes up the public

and communal praise of the Christian community reflects the impact of the one Spirit who gives diverse "gifts." It is a salutary reminder that the Spirit produces not conformity but diversity, not repetition but novelty and variation. Within the community as within creation, the Spirit calls forth a spirited abundance and diversity of life forms.

Because of this abundance, the following catalogue of acts of praise cannot be exhaustive but only indicative of the larger families of praise. That such a listing is at all possible is due to the fact that the Spirit who calls forth abundance is nevertheless a spirit of order, not of chaos. This "order" that characterizes the Spirit's enlivening presence and that distinguishes it from the feverish imitation of life is also expressed in the "repetition" of acts of praise. The doxology, the Gloria Patri, and similar songs of praise are universal in the Church of Jesus. The use of these "forms" is not—or ought not to be—the slavish perpetuation of an empty routine. Instead the presence of common and familiar forms may testify to the unity of community across generations, and to the bridging of the differences in communities. As we have seen, praise requires community. The use of "traditional forms" need not be the enemy of a proper and lively spontaneity, but may instead provide a focus for that spontaneity, a common vehicle for the expression of gratitude and joy.

Like our discussion of prayer, our discussion of praise will concentrate upon the public and communal forms which this activity takes. This means that our consideration of praise as adoration will not be concerned with the private and inward contemplation of the Godhead. We will also omit (but for a different reason) a consideration of the Lord's Supper, which is often properly termed "the Eucharist" because of its character as an act of thanksgiving and an offering of praise (the latter notion coming to the fore in the mass). The issues raised by a consideration of this activity are so vast and complex (as indicated even by the diversity of terms for it) that they require postponement and thorough explanation in a separate study. But insofar as this form of our worship has the character of praise, thanksgiving, and offering, it will share the characteristics that are under discussion here.

A. PRAISE AS ADORATION

Praise is, in the first place, a rejoicing in God, a delighting in God, the enjoyment of God. To our ears, conditioned as they are to the rhetoric of obedience and endurance, this characteristic form of praise seems odd and forced. Yet in the Gloria Patri, the doxology, and many of the hymns of our churches, this is the content and direction of praise—praise as the adoration of God.

Some people find it presumptuous to praise God, and superfluous to "glorify" him. After all, what need has God of our praise; what need has God or our feeble attempts to "laud and magnify his name"? The answer is that of course God has no need of our praise. He is not some petty tyrant who requires flattery and regular ego-pampering. We will never understand praise if we insist on attempting to fit it into categories of use and need.

Praise flows from abundance rather than need—it is characterized by enjoyment rather than use. The presence of God's Spirit is the presence in us of God's own exuberance and joy, his energy and vitality. Through the Spirit we have a share in God's joy; God's mirth roars in our veins and we are alive and enlivened. In praise as adoration, we join in and reflect the joy of God.

From the way many Christians live, one would think that the Westminster Catechism asserted that "the chief end of man is to glorify God and *endure* him forever" rather than "*enjoy* him forever." To enjoy means to put away all categories of use, need, and obligation, and to delight in divine joy, to be caught up in its contagious spirit.

Here, then, is no place for a sanctimonious solemnity. In the adoration of God, the enjoyment of God, we share for a moment in the dance of the first-born of creation. This accounts for the way in which the texts of praise as adoration often consist of superlative upon superlative in rhythmic repetition. In this way the acts of praise clearly exhibit an almost playful character.

It must be emphasized that in considering praise as adoration we are not concerned with wordless or mystical contemplation. *We are concerned not with a state to be attained but*

with public acts to be performed. It is only as public word and
deed that adoration enters into the life of the worshipping
community and so forms both the worship and the life of that
community. This is not to denigrate the traditions of mystical
contemplation of Western and Eastern Christianity, but to
deny the position of primacy often ascribed to these mystical
traditions. Acts of praise, including acts of praise as adoration,
are primarily and fundamentally communal and public in
character.

This is expressed in the phrases abounding in the texts of
praise that summon not only the community but the whole of
creation and "all the company of heaven" to join in praising
and glorifying God. It is impossible to adore "God alone" for
the simple reason that God does not "exist" alone, does not
will to be alone, but rather comes to us as the creator of heaven
and earth, who acts to save and transform the whole of creation into a new heaven and a new earth. Anyone engaging
in mystical contemplation must always be on guard, lest the
activity reverse and revoke the action, election, and promise
of God, making God devoid of creation and thus a false god.
The majesty and glory of God consist not in God's separation
from the world but in his creation and preservation, his reconciliation and redemption of the world. This is the reason
why the true adoration of God requires a company of voices—
indeed, the companionship of the whole of creation. This
truth is appropriately expressed in the public and corporate
character of praise as adoration.

But in praise as adoration we are responding not to a multiplicity of benefits but to the unity of the Giver, who in giving
us much gives us only himself. Thus acts of praise as adoration consist not in an enumeration of benefits (which is the
function of thanksgiving) but in the celebration of the one gift
that comes to us in many gifts. Adoration, then, is concerned
with God himself, with the enjoyment of the joy of God,
which is expressed in hymns of glory, praise, and honor.

A further confusion involving adoration in particular and
praise in general must be dispelled here. It arises from the
supposition that to adore God it is necessary or appropriate to
abase oneself, to defame oneself—in short, that God is en-
riched through our impoverishment. Though this idea has long

been prevalent in the church, it is nevertheless a total and fatal misconception. Abasement does have a role in confession and repentance: in that context it is the outward form of our inward need, and so gives expression to the character of prayer. It is, however, totally out of place in adoration particularly and in praise generally.[1] Abasement rests upon the logic of scarcity, which reasons that the advantage of one entails the disadvantage of the other. Insofar as our acts of praise are infected by this logic, they are akin to the barbaric flattery of a petty tyrant. Such an infection of praise may, in some situations, have effectively undermined the pretensions of earthly tyrannies, and so exerted a liberating influence. When a tyrant or one of the "princes" of the church abased himself along with his "subjects," these people may have felt somehow edified. Yet this edification has exacted a terrible price by applying the logic of scarcity to the acts of praise.

Praise is the expression of abundance, and adoration is the articulation of the divine abundance that has come to us in the outpouring of the Spirit. God's coming to us in no way impoverishes us; it enriches us. Our praise of God is not something we do "at our expense" but is the celebration of an abundance and an exuberance in which our joy mirrors the divine joy.[2]

---

[1] For a counter-argument, see Aquinas, *Summa Theologica*, II, II, Q. 84, Art. 2, pp. 1553f.

[2] The disfiguring of praise with abasement provides the (illegitimate) legitimation of theories of "religion as alienation" deriving from Feuerbach. Feuerbach's thesis is that the positive qualities of human being are first "dis-owned" and then "transferred" to (projected onto) God, who is then the creation of self-alienating imagination. He then proposes that we re-appropriate for humanity those characteristics that have been ascribed to God (and thus expropriated from us). That religion is this alienation is true to the extent to which its practice requires the impoverishment of humanity to enrich God. But this is not Christian faith which celebrates the bestowal of divine excess upon us. It is in this connection that the Eastern churches' emphasis upon salvation as deification may be seen to be far nearer the truth than all the tradition that falsely and fatally connects abasement with adoration.

I have said that abasement and renunciation have a certain place in confession. But this is the renunciation of false and illusory self-valuation in favor of the valuation that comes from God. While this process may involve replacing (false) positive qualities with negative ones, it does *not* involve ascribing these illusory qualities to God. That would be scant praise

B. PRAISE AS THANKSGIVING

In thanksgiving our praise of God, our delight in God becomes specific and detailed. That praise takes on this complexity and concreteness must not be interpreted as a lessening of the "purity" of praise. To be sure, our praise and thanksgiving expresses our joy in, and gratitude for, "one thing": that God is God in such a way that he is God with us and for us. But this "one thing" is not something among others or in place of all others. As the coming of God it is the comprehensive transformation of death into life, of brokenness into wholeness, of the old creation into the new creation. It is in this way, and only in this way, that the reign of God comes. This is the reason that the transformation of water into wine, the healing of the sick, and the feeding of the five thousand are signs of this reign and rule. They are not isolated instances of "supernatural power"; that is the stuff of superstition. They are instead the beginning of the fundamental transformation of *all* things that attest to and manifest the one thing: the coming of God's reign, the accomplishment of God's aim, the hallowing of God's name.

Thanksgiving, then, is the concrete and detailed articulation of this transformation. In thanksgiving we express the enlivening of our lives in the world, just as in prayers of petition we express the godlessness and godforsakenness of our life in the world. In both petition and thanksgiving we are concerned with the detailed and specific signs of the absence and the presence of God.

In formulating the words of thanksgiving for congregational worship, it is therefore important to name concretely and realistically those ways in which our lives are "spirited" by God's presence. Since thanksgiving is addressed to God and not to the congregation, it is important to avoid homiletical instructions about what "should" make us grateful. Thanksgiving must bring to expression in recognizable ways

---

indeed. We abandon the worthless currency of self-esteem to receive the true currency of God's esteem; we do not project our worthless currency onto God. Unfortunately, the impression that religion involves this last activity is made by ill-conceived acts of praise that inappropriately link adoration with abasement.

that which actually does give us joy—which means avoiding the tendency to "spiritualize" thanksgiving. We must not disdain the bodily and worldly in favor of some imagined "spiritual gifts." Just as in petition we name our actual and everyday needs, so in thanksgiving we name our actual and everyday joys.

In our complex and distracting world, we may of course lose track of our joy and gratitude, just as we may not be able to distinguish our actual needs from the many fabricated needs of a consumer society. In a world in which "Joy" is the name of a soap and "Luv" is the name of a truck, it is small wonder we are bewildered. Thus it is a highly important theological task that is undertaken by a pastor or another who seeks to lead a congregation or a household in thanksgiving.

For what are we actually thankful? This is a question that cannot be separated from the question, to whom are we thankful? Thanksgiving directs our ordinary and everyday joy to God—but to which God? To the promoter of our causes, or to the One who causes the sun to shine upon the just and the unjust? To an anonymous supreme being, or to the Father of Jesus? To the grantor of our wishes, or to the One who raises the dead? These questions do not undermine the realism and concreteness of the question, what actually gives us joy? Rather, the theological question (to whom are we thankful?) helps to clarify this empirical question by helping us to distinguish joy from envy and gratitude from greed. The gifts of God do not make us anxious about getting and keeping, nor do they feed this anxiety. But often we may think we are grateful when in fact we are anxious to possess, to maintain, to succeed. Asking to whom we are thankful helps us to distinguish liveliness from feverish excitement, to learn the difference between stones and bread, to distinguish joy from avarice. Joy comes not from "more of the same," which can only feed our anxiety, but from that "more than enough" which liberates us from anxiety.

Our thanksgiving is a giving of thanks "in Jesus' name" and "for Jesus' sake." It is in the life and destiny of Jesus that the Christian community discerns both the presence of God and the perfecting of human joy. It is this history which provides the test that determines whether our thanks is directed to the true God. In this "testing" we have no reason to fear that our actual and everday joy will be stolen from us and replaced with something less (under the guise of "more spiritual" joy). Jesus comes not to deprive us of our joys but "that your joy may be full" (John 15:11).

That in all things we are to give thanks (I Thess. 5:18) is true on the basis of the transformation of all things inaugurated in Jesus' life and, above all, in his resurrection. If we keep this always in mind we will not be led into the distortion of thanksgiving that teaches people to be thankful for all things. To give thanks *in* all things is not the same as giving thanks *for* all things. There exists in some of our churches an unnatural and unholy piety that attributes to God all manner of evil and destruction, and tells people that they ought to be thankful for that which is obviously destructive and *dis*spiriting. In their haste to attest to God's greatness (his omnipotence, for example), they make God a monstrosity and transform joy into a grim tribute rendered unto a petty tyrant.

What the gifts of God are like is made clear in the life and destiny of Jesus, who comes not to afflict and make captive but to give sight to the blind, deliverance to the captive. God's presence is not made evident by the crippling of those who walk but by the walking of those who are lame. If "all things work together for good," it is not the case that all things are in and of themselves "good"; rather, it is that nothing, however evil, can ultimately "separate us from the love of God in Christ Jesus" (Rom. 8:39). It is this alone that makes it possible to "give thanks in all things" and to do so truly in the name and for the sake of Jesus.[3]

---

[3]Clarity at this point will help us to understand the logic of Paul's argument in Romans 5:1-5:

> Therefore since we are justified by faith we have peace with God through our Lord Jesus Christ. Through him we have obtained access to this grace in which we stand and we rejoice in the *hope* of sharing the glory of God. More than that we rejoice in our sufferings, knowing that suffering produces endurance and endurance produces character, and character produces hope, and *hope* does not disappoint us, because God's love has been poured into our hearts through the Holy Spirit which has been given us.

That we "rejoice in our suffering" is often linked with the assertion that it "builds character." This would be a stoic argument, and it is one that Paul uses here—but its meaning is changed by the reference to *hope* which immediately precedes and follows it. It is because of that for which we hope that even *in* suffering (not *for* suffering) we may rejoice. Moreover, this hope is not mere wishful thinking, because it is grounded in the action of

Like prayer, praise takes on the actual texture of our daily lives. Praise does so by taking the form of thanksgiving, which is founded in the discernment of God's presence and the Spirit's abundance in the everyday course of our lives. God's grace does not come to us alone and apart, but is "incarnate" in and through the world of people and nature, of history and community. Thanksgiving teaches us to see—to see this face, this food, this sunset, this smile as the means of God's grace, as God's gift in which we also receive God himself. Thus thanksgiving is our response to the particularizing of God's grace—to the way in which God's love takes on earthly form and flesh to encounter us where and as we are. Thus in "all things" we give thanks "in Jesus' name" and "for Jesus' sake."

C. PRAISE AS REJOICING

In praise we not only give thanks for the way in which God has come to us but also rejoice in God's coming to all. We offer our praise not on behalf of ourselves alone but on behalf of our sisters and brothers and for all of creation. This rejoicing thus corresponds to the intercessory character of our prayer.

We rejoice in the life and liveliness of others because we know that true life and liveliness comes only from the Spirit's enlivening presence. The joy of others no less than our own is the sure sign that God has not abandoned or forgotten his world but has come and does come to his creatures. The joy of others is infectious because it is the clear witness that we are not alone and that our hope is not in vain. Accordingly, the joys of others are our joys as well.

This would be impossible if there were in fact "less than enough." In the kingdom of scarcity, the joy of one is the sorrow of another, and thus the root of envy, bitterness, and resentment. But from the prespective of faith, the joy of another is the sign—even in the midst of scarcity and anxiety—of an abundance that is "more than enough." We rejoice in

---

God (through our Lord Jesus Christ) and in the presence of God (through the Holy Spirit). So powerful is God's action and presence that our suffering cannot be a final obstacle to our joy but is in fact turned to good account through our hope, so that we may rejoice even in suffering. There is here, then, neither a masochistic reveling in pain nor a stoic acceptance of it, but an eschatological transformation of it.

the joy of others not out of some imagined altruism, but because the presence of joy attests to an abundance that overcomes all scarcity and therefore also our poverty and lack. This is why we may and must speak, as Paul does, of rejoicing with those who rejoice (Rom. 12:15), just as we also speak of mourning with those who mourn and of "bearing one another's burdens."

We must understand that this rejoicing may not restrict itself in any arbitrary or suspicious fashion—we rejoice "with those who rejoice." It is the joy and liveliness and spiritedness of the other for which we rejoice, even when this individual is not of our group, our class, our community. Even when an individual does not realize that this joy derives from God's Spirit and thus from God's action, we may and must rejoice in this joy. There is no room here for the mistrust and stingy discrimination between the righteous and the unrighteous, for rejoicing with the former but being suspicious of the joy of the latter. True Christian freedom is freedom from envy, even the "spiritual" envy that puts so much stake in the discrimination between righteous and unrighteous. That an individual is ignorant of the true basis of the joy that he or she experiences is of no consequence for us here. (It has consequences for proclamation and witness, but not for praise, thanksgiving, and rejoicing.) We know that basis, and because and insofar as we know this the joy of the other is not an occasion for envy or reproach but for gratitude and rejoicing.

So far as I can see, this is the only basis for the continuing involvement of representatives of the church in the "celebration" of the marriage of those who are not specifically rooted in the community, or in the celebration of birth that has so often become (erroneously) the content of infant baptism. These otherwise very dubious practices have their relative legitimation in the fact that as Christians we rejoice with those who rejoice.

It is pointless to complain that the joy of these others is undoubtedly infected with a certain egotism and self-centeredness, and therefore with greed and unbelief. Of course this is true, but it is true not only for them but also for us. It is all the more true for us if we let the dubious character of the other's joy excuse us from rejoicing with him or her. What we should remember is the verse about being offended by the speck in the eye of the other without noticing that we are blinded by the beam in our own. Imagined righteousness is nothing but self-righteousness, which can only envy those who rejoice, not rejoice with them.

We *especially* need to beware of the "spiritualizing" and egoistic tendency to rejoice only with the joy of the other who hears the Gospel and thus joins with the community of praise. This is indeed a cause for great rejoicing, not only for us but "for all the company of heaven." But I have often noticed that in our churches we apply this saying about the rejoicing over the finding of one who has been lost (Luke 15:10) in such a way that we excuse ourselves from rejoicing with others who rejoice but who are not yet redeemed. We must not forget at this point that the Spirit is the Spirit of life and the gift of the Spirit is joy, and that it is only because this is so that the Spirit is the Spirit of Christ. Thus we rejoice not only on account of the "conversion" of another but at any and all other manifestations of abundant life in another.[4]

We must not give the impression in our public praise and thanksgiving that the Spirit is a cultic or tribal spirit who gives life and joy only to our community—that for which we hope is the pouring out of the Spirit upon *all* flesh. Like our own joys, the joys of our neighbor are the provisional and limited but nevertheless real and actual accomplishment of that for which we hope. When asked if he was the Messiah, Jesus did not reply, Look how many believe, look how many have joined, see how many call me Lord; rather, he said, "The lame walk, the blind receive their sight . . ." (Luke 7:22-3). In all the joys of all those who rejoice, we, too—in Jesus' name and for his sake—join in their rejoicing.

D. PRAISE AS OFFERING

Praise is not only verbal—it is physical, embodied in the action of the community. We not only lift up our voices in songs

---

[4]"It could not be the joy referred to in Philippians if it were unable or unwilling to rejoice in the truth even when it encounters it in sinners and therefore to 'rejoice with them that do rejoice' (Rom. 12:13)" (Barth, *Church Dogmatics,* III/2, p. 284).

of praise but also "bring offerings," giving out of the abundance that we have received. The moment in our common worship that we call the "offering" or "offertory" is a continuation and expression of our praise and thanksgiving. Indeed, it is the culmination and climax of praise, for through this action we demonstrate that abundance and exuberance that has come to us not only in general but in particular, not only "spiritually" but also physically.

It is at this point that it is particularly important to recall that God comes to us in the actual worldliness and bodiliness of our existence, that we receive from God both the kingdom and "our daily bread." We receive in abundance and "more than enough" because we receive from the one who promises, and gives, himself. It is therefore out of thanks for the concrete abundance of what we have received that we make our offering.

Much misunderstanding is generated by the connection between "offering" and "sacrifice" and the associations that we bring to the idea of "sacrifice." This connection and association introduces a completely false and necessarily fatal element into the character of our offering and therefore into our praise. We have come to think of sacrifice as a giving-up of what is basically "not enough," a giving that is thus somehow costly and even overburdening. Ministers and others often rather drearily and even incessantly reinforce this misconception by hammering away at the themes of "stewardship" and tithing. This emphasis produces the distorted notion that the offering, far from being an exuberant expression of thanks, is the extortion of a kind of tax. This kind of offering is all too clearly motivated by guilt and fear rather than joy and gratitude.

In certain religious practices, worshippers offer sacrifices to a god to appease him or to gain his favor. But such sacrifice and offering sometimes takes on the character of an exuberant "potlatch" that manifests the excess and abundance which is the fruit of the Sacred.[5] In Christianity there is no longer any possibility for sacrifice in the first sense. We do not have an

---

[5]For a description of the "potlatch" of the Kwakiutl, cf. Ruth Benedict, *Patterns of Culture* (Houghton Mifflin, 1934), pp. 195-211.

angry or arbitrary deity to appease nor a greedy or reluctant deity to be cajoled, because we worship the one whose grace is more abundant than all our need and whose mercy over-flows all bounds. Thus, if our offering is grim and grudging, we can only be presenting it to a god other than the one who has come to us in Jesus and is present to us as the Spirit. Consequently, God's people should not be cajoled or "moti-vated" to give up what is already "less than" or "only enough." We can only offer our abundance, gladly and exuberantly.

The story of Cain and Abel found in Genesis 4 is an es-pecially pertinent one here. Cain's catastrophic error was re-garding his sacrifice as an earning of favor rather than as a response to grace already granted. With this view of his sac-rifice he was immediately at odds with his brother Abel, be-cause where there is favor to be earned there is less than enough, and where there is scarcity there is envy. In fact, Abel's murder was implicit in Cain's sacrifice, because Cain sought to gain an advantage in a system of "scarce goods." That Cain was unable to rejoice in Abel's joy is but a further indication of the fatal distortion that was involved in Cain's sacrifice. In the Church we must ask ourselves if we are mak-ing Cain's sacrifice or Abel's offering.

We should remind ourselves that this abundance is not a matter of quantity; it is a matter of Spirit. It is the Spirit's presence that makes whatever we have "more than enough." And the absence of that Spirit will render our "much"—how-ever great—still less than enough. It is as and when the en-livening Spirit is present that praise and thanksgiving also take the form of an offering given out of abundance.

In the order of our worship we express our joy and gratitude in particular acts of praise. The ordering of these acts is the liturgy, the work of the people," which includes the elements of adoration, thanksgiving, rejoicing, and offering. It is through these forms that the members of the community present unto God their lives in all aspects—their response to the one who gives life and liveliness and therefore abundant life.

CHAPTER SIX
Praise as Formation

"Praise always," says Paul (I Thess. 5:16); "Give thanks in all things" (I Thess. 5:18) is an admonition with the same meaning. These injunctions are parallel to the admonition to "pray without ceasing." To "praise always" does not mean to set aside more time for acts of praise or to offer praise more often and more regularly. No matter how often we stopped what we were doing to sing praises, it would never amount to "always." Thus, admonitions to give praise and thanks with greater regularity or earnestness are completely beside the point here.

Moreover, such admonitions to praise more often, like those to pray more often, succeed only in extending the display of a "religiosity" that Christian faith seeks to overcome. We cannot become more Christian by becoming more religious. As Christians we await a new heaven and a new earth, not the escape from the old earth into the old heaven, or the colonization of the old earth by the old heaven.

Like the admonition to "pray without ceasing," the admonition to "praise always" describes a way of life. Both are summarized by the exhortation to "present your bodies as a reasonable worship" (Rom. 12:1). As we have seen, the term "body" here refers to the way we live in the world, to the visible or public set of relationships that make up our life. It is our life with others; our life in community; our life as work and play, as social, cultural, political, and economic connectedness; our life as the life of nature. It is thus our everyday life that Paul characterizes as praise, just as he has characterized this life as prayer.

To "praise always," then, will mean that our lifestyle will somehow express that same joy and gratitude that we shape into hymns of praise and thanksgiving in our common worship.[1] The ways in which praise may shape our lifestyle are as diverse as the ways in which our hymns express praise. When we speak of lifestyle, we are not talking about uniformity or conformity to an external law; we are talking about the real diversity that reflects the diversity of the "gifts of the Spirit," the diversity of ways in which we have been spirited. The lifestyle that we fashion is our expression of this "spiriting," this enlivening.

This diversity, however, is not the chaotic disarray of a feverish imitation of life and Spirit; it is the consciously formed and styled diversity of community. Accordingly, it is possible to identify in this diversity some of the common themes that characterize life shaped like praise.

We sometimes ask ourselves, Why am I here? what is the purpose and meaning of life? The Westminster Catechism asks the same question in somewhat more archaic language: "What is the chief end of man?" We know many answers to this question, answers given us by our friends, by our society, by contending ideologies. But we also implicitly answer this question through the lifestyle we choose or "fall into." The answer that the Westminster Catechism proposes is straight forward: "The chief end of man is to glorify God and enjoy him forever." Notice that it does *not* tell me to obey God or to serve God, nor does it tell me to be a useful member of society—still less to work or to be a good citizen, to do my duty. It tells me "to enjoy."

For some reason this is a very difficult word for us to hear. Much of our life is governed by the necessity to work, to earn our way, to make something of ourselves, to do good, to gain respect and acceptability. And this way of living carries over into our relationship with God: we attempt to placate his wrath, avoid his judgment, earn his love, gain his favor. But all of this is what Paul called "justification by works." It is sheer unbelief, an arrogant refusal of the Gospel.

A lifestyle shaped like praise and thanksgiving is, above all,

---

[1] It is in this connection that we can understand Paul's otherwise obscure admonition: "Glorify God in your body" (I Cor. 6:20). In this sense it would mean to glorify and give praise to God in one's way of living in the world.

a lifestyle that corresponds to the abundance of grace.[2] As such, this life is the life of an individual who has been set free from bondage to necessity and scarcity. It is therefore the life of a person free to enjoy—not to use and be used but to enjoy and rejoice, to enjoy God and all God's works. This person is therefore free to laugh and dance and sing like the first-born of God's new creation.

Such a way of life is directly counter to our habitual way of living in the world, that is, grasping, seizing, holding—in short, being anxious.

A. FROM ANXIETY TO ASSURANCE

Perhaps nothing Jesus said is as foreign to us as his admonition to "be not anxious" (Matt. 6:25). Our life is built upon the habit of anxiety. To exist without anxiety about what we will eat or wear, without "taking thought for the morrow," is almost unthinkable for us. Our life is most often an endless succession of various attempts to control tomorrow, to assure our future well-being. We buy insurance, pay social security, save for a "rainy day." Often we defer truly living today in the hope that tomorrow we will *really* live. We postpone life, freedom, and self-determination until we graduate, until we get married, until the children are grown, until we retire. Suddenly our time is gone, and we have postponed life—indefinitely. We have spent our days getting ready to live, a terrible cost to allow anxiety to exact from us.

To the extent to which our anxiety is an attempt to avert or postpone death, death rules our life.[3] The very measures

[2]So according to Gerhard von Rad: "Praising and not praising stand over against one another like life and death: praise becomes the most elementary 'mark of being alive.'" (*Old Testament Theology*, Vol. I, Eng. tr. [Harper & Row, 1968], p. 370). Jürgen Moltmann comments: "We have our life in praising God, hoping in him and giving thanks to him" (*The Theology of Hope*, Eng. tr. [Harper & Row, 1967], p. 209). It then remains to ask, as we proceed to do now, what this means for life. (Cf. Barth, *Church Dogmatics*, III/2, pp. 166-174.) It was only after I completed my book that I obtained a copy of Geoffrey Wainwright's *Doxology: The Praise of God in Worship, Doctrine, and Life* (Oxford, 1980). Wainwright's discussion is excellent—useful and provocative—and I recommend it to readers of this book.

[3]See Ernest Becker, *The Denial of Death* (Free Press, 1974) for a discussion of the way in which death rules life in the very process of our attempting to avoid death.

that we take to avert it give it greater control over our lives, and our anxiety increases rather than decreases. Every anxious defense only surrenders another hostage to anxiety, thereby increasing its power and threat.

It is precisely in this context that Jesus' admonition—"Be not anxious"—has such pertinence and validity. With this word Jesus releases us from bondage to the iron law of necessity and care, because he assures us that our life is given us by God, who gives us all we need. Jesus himself is this assurance, something we proclaim whenever we claim that he is Lord, that in and through him God has come to us and has acted on our behalf. To the extent to which this is true, anxiety becomes alien to us. And lest we forget that we are thus liberated and thus permitted to be carefree, we are commanded, "Be not anxious."

Of course, we are beset by all our old anxieties despite Jesus's assurance, and in the name of "responsibility" we justify our anxiety by saying, "Surely Jesus does not ask us to be carefree and irresponsible." After all, we have work to do, children to raise, a church to build. And so, sometimes even in the name of faith, we bind ourselves once again to the treadmill of anxiety. This is the reason why it is so terribly dangerous not to recognize the scope and radical nature of Jesus' admonition. In truth we are invited and summoned to a life that will be irresponsible and carefree by the world's definition. We must remember that Christian responsibility and worldly responsibility are two different things. The world will hold us to its own laws, its own necessities, but only to the extent to which we respond to this pressure will we be permitted to feel "responsible." If our existence is a response to God's grace, we will not respond to those pressures that the world uses to try to ensnare us in its version of responsibility. So long as we do nothing that family and friends, church and state regard as irresponsible, we will not have responded to God's grace "which overcomes the world."

We are called, then, to what may be termed responsible irresponsibility—"responsible" because it is a knowing response to God's grace, not a blind bondage to fleeting whims; and "irresponsibility" because this response may oppose the ways in which the world tries to ensnare us in its own version

of what is necessary or important. To the world, which counsels us to be anxious about tomorrow, to prepare for it, we
may appear irresponsibly carefree. To be sure, the pressures
of our earthly life will always be great, and our existence will
often enough be characterized by need, lack, and yearning.
But insofar as our existence is shaped like and formed by
praise, it will be marked by noticeable assurance and an apparent irresponsibility.

The specific form of this freedom from anxiety will vary
considerably from person to person. For some it may take the
form of "dropping out" of the ordinary responsibilities of life.
Refusing medical treatment when it can no longer cure, refusing wealth, choosing celibacy—these are all dramatic ways
in which this "positive irresponsibility" may take shape in our
lives. It may also take less dramatic forms—feasting instead
of dieting, resting instead of jogging, playing instead of working. Above all, it will take the form of a sense of humor, a
general sense of well-being that cannot be constrained by the
grim and sober face of anxiety. We will all find different ways
to express in our lives this assurance, this end of anxiety, this
positive irresponsibility. Insofar as we have been "spirited,"
our "irresponsibility" will be irrepressible. It is only a matter
of finding the proper words and actions with which to give it
form and focus in the kind of life we live.

One place where this must take place is in the life of the
church. In far too many ways the church only increases anxiety and care, and so contradicts itself as a community of
praise and thanksgiving. This anxiety is evident not only in
the threat of "hellfire" but also in our preoccupation with the
survival, the extension, and even the reform of the institution.
If life in the church is governed by anxiety, we need also to
be liberated from responsibility to the church. I am not talking
about rebelling against the church or leaving it—these are
only reactionary measures that leave us in bondage to the
necessities of rebellion. What I mean is that a believer with
a lifestyle formed by corporate praise and thanksgiving will
usually find it impossible to take the church (its rules, its
programs, its institutional necessities) as seriously as the
church, in its self-preoccupation, takes itself.

Above all, we must be released from anxiety before God.

To the extent to which we seek to placate God's wrath, avoid God's judgment, earn God's favor—to that extent we refuse to believe God. To the extent to which God becomes a means to our ends, a way to get what we want, a way to insure our life, a way to tranquilize our anxiety—to that extent we are worshipping an idol. All of these responses are the way of religiosity, of faithless piety. If God has come to us in our godlessness, then we have nothing to earn. We are adopted as sons and daughters, not sold into unending slavery. We may therefore live "before God as if there were no God" (Bonhoeffer).[4] That is, we may enjoy and rejoice in God's favor and presence with no thought for the religious idols of church or world. To the extent to which we know that God has come to us and is for us—to that extent we are free from anxiety before God.

B. LIFE WITH THE OTHER

When our need is overwhelmed by God's grace, when our anxiety is flooded with assurance, when our godlessness is invaded by the Spirit, then our life with our neighbor is also transformed. In our need and our poverty, we often see our neighbor as a competitor, a threat. In our scramble to get enough food, enough power, enough meaning, enough love, enough security, we see our neighbor as either a means to use for our ends or a threat to our "happiness." Only if she will be like us, an aid to us, will she not be our enemy. But this means that we must deprive our neighbor of her independence, and thus we become her enemy. When this kind of enmity rules our relationships, it sometimes erupts in violence. More often it expresses itself in less dramatic ways: we do not have to destroy our neighbor if we can use and manipulate her. Friends, lovers, parents, and children get trapped in this quiet and even decorous routine of secret enmity and resentment.

These feelings are the fruit of our anxious grasping for enough, of our anxious attempt to establish our own life, to be the source of our own existence. But when God's presence

---

[4]Bonhoeffer, *Letters and Papers from Prison*, p. 219.

and gracious action overwhelms our anxiety, then our neighbor looks different to us; we see him as a gift, and therefore as a true neighbor.

A lifestyle shaped by praise and thanksgiving is embodied in the unconditional welcome of the other as neighbor. It does not depend upon our determining whether this other is friend or enemy; the very possibility of such a distinction is overwhelmed. It is in this light that we can understand Jesus' injunction to love the enemy (Luke 6:35) as the straightforward clarification of the command to love one's neighbor. Friend and enemy alike are neighbors because they are the gift of God's love whereby God himself comes to us. Our neighbor is a gift because she invades our isolation, rescuing us (disregarding the distinction between friend and enemy) from the self-imposed solitary confinement of anxiety.

Perhaps in this way we may gain new insight into one of Jesus' most bewildering stories: the parable of the good Samaritan (Luke 10:29-36). Like most of Jesus' stories, this one utterly defies any attempt to reduce it to a straightforward thesis. The more familiar it is, the more bizarre it seems. "Love your neighbor as yourself," says Jesus. "Who is my neighbor?" asks a listener. Jesus then tells the story of a man who is robbed and left for dead, of those "friends" who pass by, and of the "enemy" who helps. At the story's end he asks, "Who was neighbor to this man?"

Notice that several things have happened here. Notice first what the story does *not* do: it does not offer the Samaritan as an illustration of what it means to love the neighbor. If that were the meaning of the story, Jesus' concluding question would be "Who loved this man?" Instead he asks, "Who was neighbor to this man?" Thus Jesus answers the question "Who am I supposed to love?" with another question. The listener asks about obligation, and Jesus answers by asking about gratitude. In this way Jesus has completely changed the frame of reference, obliterating the distinction between ally and enemy.

The best way to describe this story is to say that it doesn't have a meaning, a moral. (Certainly the Samaritan isn't a model to be emulated. After all, he is the neighbor—isn't he?) Rather, the story does something. It turns the listener upside down, changing his question (what do I have to do and to whom?) into a response (gratitude for being rescued).

The other is my neighbor, obliterating categories of ally and enemy; the other is a gift. Engaging in a bit of dangerous allegory, I can explain it this way. You and I have fallen into a band of robbers, and we live in secret enmity and resentment. We divide the world into allies and enemies, but resentment is the law ruling both—the same law that leads us to ask, what do I have to do to be saved? This is the wilderness in which we are battered and bloodied and left for dead. Here a neighbor finds us, but who is this neighbor? A friend? No, a Samaritan, one whose very existence opposes my own, who lives outside of and against the law, outside of and against my national and religious identity. A Samaritan is to a good Jew what a communist is to a capitalist—surely not an ally. An enemy, then? No, he binds my wounds. Who, then, is this neighbor who is neither ally nor enemy? Is he another person? Is he God, or Jesus? Perhaps he is all of these.

The law that governs my relation to the other is either one of grasping (and therefore enmity and resentment) or one of gratitude. In the first case I have no neighbor—only allies and enemies. In the second case I have no allies and enemies—only neighbors. For in the second case my need has been overwhelmed by abundance, my grasping by gratitude, my resentment by rejoicing. When God has come to us in Jesus, the other is a gift, and therefore a neighbor to be welcomed (Rom. 15:7).

In *Life Together* Dietrich Bonhoeffer remarked that the things about my brother or sister that especially offend me are the very things that mark my sister and brother as God's gift to me.[5] This assertion must seem very odd indeed, until we see it in the light of the other as gift. It is precisely the otherness of my neighbor, his strangeness, that marks him as "not myself." This otherness is experienced in two basic ways. If there is less than enough, if life is competition under the law of enmity, then the other as "not me" is my enemy; the

[5]Cf. Dietrich Bonhoeffer, *Life Together*, Eng. tr. (Harper & Row, 1954), p. 28.

difference between him and me offends and threatens me.[6] I resent it, am irritated by it. What most annoys me about my friend is the way in which he acts "out of character," the way in which he does not conform to my fantasy, my "script."

Though it is precisely this irreducible otherness that offends me, it is also this "difference" that is the sign to me that I am not alone—not alone with my fantasy, my fear, my hall of mirrors. It is exactly that which offends and exasperates me that is God's gift to me, that invades my self-imposed exile into anxiety and enmity. It is for this reason that the other (whether friend or enemy) is a neighbor to be welcomed in joy and gratitude. Her otherness becomes the sign that we are not alone, but have been encountered by one we thought alien, and rescued. Since God has come to us and has acted for us, the other as other has become our neighbor. Since God has become our neighbor in Jesus, all persons have become our neighbors. In fact, God gives himself to us by giving us neighbors. Thus our love of God and our love of our neighbor are together embodied as praise and thanksgiving. This is the fulfillment of the law. It is for this that we may live.

From this vantage point the meaning of the commandments becomes self-evident. Far from being a strange and limiting obligation, the law is itself the sign of this gift and grace. To the extent to which our need has been overwhelmed by grace, covetousness is simply unthinkable. How is envy possible if we know in our hearts and see in reality that there really is more than enough? How is murder possible if the other is my neighbor? How is adultery, the desire to possess another, any longer imaginable? When Jesus broadens the commandment against murder to include hatred and resentment, when he broadens the comandment against adultery to include lustful desire, he clarifies the true basis of the law in the Gospel.

The "law" makes it abundantly clear that existence is founded upon grace. If the law is appropriated as obligation, as necessity, as a means to establishing existence, then it is an alien intrusion, a dreadful prison. Then indeed must sal-

---

[6]For a somewhat more extended discussion, cf. T. W. Jennings, "Human Sexuality: A Theological Perspective" in *Journal of Pastoral Care*, March 1979.

vation come to us, as Paul says, apart from the law (Rom. 3:21). But if the law is the signpost to existence founded in the gracious and enlivening onrush of God's Spirit, then it is itself the sign of God's gift. In this last sense we may understand what Jesus means when he says, "I have come not to abolish but to fulfill" the law (Matt. 5:17). The law is fulfilled not by obedience to an obligation but by gratitude for that gift that overcomes all our fear and anxiety. As the one in whom God comes to us and gives himself to us and for us, Jesus is the fulfillment of the law—in person. He has become the basis for our love of God and our neighbor—he in whom God has come to us as our neighbor.

A lifestyle shaped by praise and thanksgiving is a lifestyle that welcomes the other as a neighbor. As such it is the transformation of resentment into rejoicing, of enmity into hospitality, of grasping into giving. Our life with our neighbor is, precisely in this way, an act of praise whereby our everyday life (our body) is itself presented as a "reasonable worship."

C. THE POLITICS OF PRAISE

To be embodied is to be engaged in a complex variety of relationships and connections with the world. Our bodiliness is what relates us. But our bodiliness is also what makes our relationships social, political, and economic. A lifestyle shaped by praise manifests itself in these dimensions, just as a lifestyle shaped by prayer means a particular kind of involvement with social, political, and economic structures.

To give praise and thanksgiving is to recognize that there is "more than enough." But such a recognition places us in direct conflict with the social, economic, and political structures of our world, which are based upon "scarcity." Economic structures are based upon a scarcity of goods, of wealth; political structures are based upon a scarcity of power; military institutions are based upon fear, the sense that security is scarce. All of these structures and institutions seek to distribute scarcity, to regulate access to some scarce good. When such structures distribute this scarcity fairly, we call them just. When they seem to over-restrict access to that which is scarce, or when they seem to be "arbitrary," we call them unjust. The injustice of any particular system is likely to be seen more vividly by those who are left out of the distribution. When this injustice is widely recognized, a group usually calls either for the adjustment of the system of distribution (reform) or for a very different system altogether (revolution). What unites systems and the calls for reform and revolution—what unites democracy and tyranny, capitalism and communism, liberals and reactionaries, reformers and revolutionaries—is the agreement that there is not enough. All agree that there is not enough food, not enough security, not enough power, not enough privilege.

No one can deny that in our world there is in fact less than enough, but this common perception is used to justify or to dismiss a staggering amount of human misery. Political and economic structures keep themselves in power by claiming that they are necessary, by pretending to be absolute. We are seduced into taking these systems as seriously as they take themselves because we fear that there is indeed less than enough.

But what happens when we suspect that there is really more than enough? What happens when we begin to act as if there is more than enough? This is precisely what we begin to do when we engage in praise and thanksgiving. We act as if there is more than enough, as though the Spirit of life and abundance has descended upon us, as if God has given us himself and so has given us more than enough. In short, we act as if we are saved "by grace."

And it doesn't stop with praise and thanksgiving. Our bodies are our reasonable worship says Paul, and so our praise and thanksgiving spill over into the way we live. Because God's coming is no merely ethereal or heavenly coming but a coming that transforms heaven and earth, this praise and thanksgiving spills over into our economic, political, and social connectedness. If it does not, then we have refused the fullness of our praise and thanksgiving, we have withheld our bodies from worship, we have restricted the coming of God.

But if praise and thanksgiving spill over into our political, social, and economic relationships, what will happen? Obviously, we will be unable to take the structures and institutions as seriously as they take themselves, unable to accept them as self-evident and necessary. Unjust structures depend upon the claim that they are self-evidently necessary, but if we are living a life of true praise and thanksgiving, we will be unable to restrain ourselves from debunking these structures, and they will begin to totter. In our own society this may mean that we debunk the self-evident necessity of the kingdom of force (militarism), the kingdom of use (consumerism), and the kingdom of scarcity (capitalism). Idols cannot survive being debunked; the devil, it is said, has no sense of humor. When praise spills over into the public arena, it may become truly "revolutionary," for it unmasks idols, debunks the "principalities and powers," and exorcises demons.

When Elijah wanted to destroy the worship of Baal, he set up a kind of game (I Kgs. 18:17-40). He proposed that they ready two stacks of wood, two offerings. Then he asked the priests of Baal to call down fire to light their offering—he taunted them, he ridiculed them and their god. They tried; they prayed, but Baal did not answer them. Elijah soaked his own woodpile with water thus adding insult to injury. When he prayed, the blaze from heaven consumed his offering, to the complete humiliation of the priests of Baal and their god. (When Elijah killed these priests, it was almost an act of mercy.) Certain people today are following Elijah's example. When students gathered in Washington, D.C., to protest the war in Vietnam, they engaged in street theater—they even attempted to levitate the Pentagon! They debunked the system. When the National Guard was called out to some campuses, demonstrators sometimes met them with flowers and kisses, a response that must have made it difficult for the soldiers to feel militaristic. When a certain black minister was arrested in South Africa by fiercely fundamentalist white police, he ordered them to repent. It is said they finally had to let him go to get any peace!

Of course, crusaders aren't always successful when they set out to debunk society's structures. There are and always will be martyrs, casualties in the war for justice, because the principalities and powers do not give up without a fight. But sometimes the martyrs go singing, and then they are truly that church against whom not even the gates of hell can prevail (Matt. 16:18). Against such fierce joy, death and the devil have no power. The trumpets of praise and thanksgiving shatter the walls of our fortified structures, of our Jerichos (Josh. 6:1-20).

In the discussion of prayer as formation, we noticed that a life shaped like prayer is a life of action and involvement. The action that imitates prayer is not itself the accomplishment of a goal but an asking and a yearning, and so it is with praise. The action in the world that imitates and is shaped by praise is not determined by a calculation of means and ends. The martyr does not go to death singing in order to cause Nero to tremble, and still less in order to bring down the empire. An act governed by praise does not accomplish liberation; it is the expression of liberation itself. It reflects the already accomplished act of liberation that has occurred in the life and destiny of Jesus. In this lies its peculiar combination of power and powerlessness. In the world's calculation, this act of praise is trivial, frivolous, and without effect; the earth's tyrants think in terms of physical force. "How many divisions does the Pope have?" asked Stalin. To which the church of the martyrs replies with irrepressible mirth: "Together with the angels and archangels and all the company of heaven, we laud and magnify thy holy name. . . ."

Public action, political and social action shaped like praise is more like a song than a task. Its peculiar power is that with its song it undermines the self-importance of every task. Even in the midst of the most terrible oppression, it is possible to act as if freedom were already more real than slavery. This I have seen both in my native Southland and in South Africa,[7] and it is true wherever the community of God lives.

D. LIFE WITH NATURE

Just as praise forms our life with our neighbor and our life in the world, it may also form our life with nature. Most of the

[7]For a contemporary illustration of this, see the memoir by Aelrod Stubbs in *Steve Biko: I Write What I Like* (Harper & Row, 1978), pp. 154-216. He and the others (Robert Sobukwe and Richard Turner) to whom this book is dedicated were so astonishing because they lived as if they were already free and gave others the power to do so as well. Cf. also Theodore W. Jennings, "Steve Biko: A Tribute," *Christian Century*, Jan. 18, 1977.

time we see nature as something to use, to exploit, to control, to tame, to fear. This is the fruit of our anxiety and our corresponding desire to control and establish our life. But if in our relationship with nature we also are met with "more than enough," with the onrush on the Spirit, then here too we may learn to shape a life that enjoys rather than controls.

"My body is that piece of the earth which I am," writes Käsemann.[8] If my body is shaped by praise, this will mean that the earth, too, is my neighbor with whom I rejoice, in whom I delight, a feeling concretely expressed in my lifestyle. If I recognize the earth as my neighbor, I cannot be oblivious to the rending of its beauty, the extermination of its species, the polluting of its air and water, the scarring of its surface. If I am to rejoice with and delight in the earth, and so give praise, I must debunk the iron necessity of ravishing the earth in the name of technology.

This is not some idle utopian fancy. Indeed, at the heart of both true art and true science stands just such a respect for and rejoicing in nature. Art that is not only appropriation and science that is not only technique are the attentive and intelligent welcoming of and rejoicing in the earth. In this way art and science are, as the Germans say, spiritual (geistliche) acts. True art and science only survive when they are freed from anxiety and pursued for truth. Then they both partake—even if hiddenly—in that rejoicing in creation which springs from a delight in God "and all his works."[9]

A lifestyle that is shaped like and formed by praise is one that gives thanks in all things. This gratitude and joy embodies itself in our way of living in the world—in our life with our neighbor, in our life in the public world of political and economic institutions, in our life with nature. Our acts of praise in our public and corporate worship are not isolated "religious" acts but the model of our life in the world. For it is

[8]"Primitive Christian Apocalyptic," New Testament Questions of Today, Eng. tr. (Fortress, 1969), p. 135.

[9]That a theology of nature properly drives from a theology of "glory" is a view put forward by Iwand and appropriated by Moltmann. For a discussion, see M. Douglas Meeks, Origins of the Theology of Hope (Fortress, 1974), pp. 30-41. Also see Moltmann, The Theology of Hope, pp. 89-91.

only as our life in the world begins to take on the shape of this praise that we begin to "give thanks in all things." The more clear and joyous our acts of praise in corporate and public worship, the more suitable they become as models for our lifestyle. Then the hymn of praise and thanksgiving of the community of Jesus becomes the *cantus firmus* that supports the melody of a lifestyle that is itself a song of praise. When our existence is so changed, our everyday life in the world—like water turned into wine—is transformed.

PART III:
A Life of Prayer and Praise

Prayer and praise are the two fundamental actions of our common worship: together in alternation they give worship its structure and rhythm. Yet they are as different from one another as night and day—and as closely related to one another. As night and day are distinguished from one another by the absence and presence of the sun, so prayer and praise are distinguished by the absence and presence of God, the same God to whom both are directed.

In this concluding chapter we will explore the relationship between prayer and praise. First we shall explore how they are related structurally or fundamentally (corresponding to our earlier discussion of their respective "shapes"). Then, just as we discussed the typical forms of prayer and praise, we will discuss their "liturgical" relationship, asking how they pattern our worship. As our worship is patterned by the alternation of prayer and praise, so may our lifestyle be structured by the alternation of a deep yearning for God and the enjoyment of God's presence and God's reign. Thus we shall see in what way the alternation between prayer and praise interprets and shapes our everyday (non-religious) existence in the world.

A. THE INTERDEPENDENCE OF PRAYER AND PRAISE

As we have noted, prayer is the expression of our yearning, our desire and need for the God who is absent, distant, or silent; praise is the expression of our joy in and gratitude for God's presence. Prayer is the expression of our life as lack, as poverty, as emptiness; praise is the expression of our life as abundant, overflowing, full, and exuberant. These different acts are complementary, and belong together.

Prayer and praise cannot be reduced to a single action, nor can their unity be expressed by a single principle. Their unity is not abstract; it is more like that of a rhythm, a story, a dance, a song—a unity that needs time. The unity of prayer and

126

praise is expressed primarily in the unity of narrative and in the unity of liturgy.

This means that we must beware of taking a "middle ground" between prayer and praise. The reduction of these to a "common denominator" is catastrophic to the understanding and practice of both. Prayer becomes associated with the sense of God's presence, an association whose consequences we have already noted. Praise is deprived of its joyful character and becomes a burden, a kind of tribute rendered to an abstract or absent-minded or tyrannical deity.

The unity of prayer and praise is not to be discovered in some "middle ground" but in the one to whom they are addressed. This is not an abstract unity but a unity "in action," discerned by Christians in the person of Jesus and especially in his destiny. In the destiny of Jesus both God's absence (the cross) and his presence (the Resurrection) are united. This is not the unity of a single moment; it is the unity of history, which cannot be displayed "all at once" but only "through time."

Similarly, the unity of prayer and praise "takes time." The basis of this unity is expressed through the story of promise and fulfillment, of Genesis and Revelation, of death and resurrection. The unity of prayer and praise is expressed in and through the action of ritual and liturgy, something that does not occur all at once but in the alternation between the words of prayer and the words of praise. Similarly, prayer and praise as the form of our lifestyle cannot be reduced to a single principle or rule. They are present not simultaneously but in an alternating rhythm, a rhythm that constitutes the form of Christian life.

Before we further explore the character of this rhythm of worship and life, it is important for us to see more clearly how prayer and praise belong together. We must see how they require and illumine one another. We shall do this by first seeing how praise is necessary for prayer, and then asking how prayer makes praise possible.

Of these two actions, praise may be understood as more fundamental, because without it prayer is impossible. Praise is the hidden presupposition of our prayer, a claim that can be made clear in a variety of ways. We may begin by recalling that both prayer and praise are dependent upon the Spirit's presence, the basis of that enlivening abundance that we express in praise and thanksgiving. Yet it is the same Spirit whose presence makes prayer possible, that calling upon God in his absence that is, as Tertullian suggests, a vanquishing of God. Apart from the Spirit, we cannot pray "as we ought," yet the Spirit is God's presence and so the basis for praise. This explanation might seem circular, but we can clarify it if we look again at the meaning of the absence and the presence of God.

We have said that prayer expresses our godlessness and godforsakenness and thus the absence of God. This absence is no mere illusion: insofar as we experience injustice, want, and brokenness, God is not present. This is, therefore, a real absence—but not an absolute absence. It is the absence of what "ought" to be there, the absence of that which is no longer present or not yet present. It is like the difference between being alone and being lonely. I am lonely when someone is no longer or not yet there; their absence is related to their presence. If I'm merely alone, then the other is not present either in memory or in hope. The absence of God is more like being lonely than like being merely alone; I must have some sense of God's presence in order to feel God's absence.

Thus we could say that God must "somehow" be present if I am to speak of his being absent. This "somehow" is an expectation, a yearning, a memory or a trace of that which is absent. Apart from this expectation, this memory of or yearning for God's presence, we would not notice or protest God's absence. Thus sensing God's absence requires the expectation of God's presence.

We may now see how the Spirit (the presence) of God is necessary for prayer as the expression of God's absence. The Spirit is the way in which God is present in us—in our yearning for or memory of God—that awakens in us a protest against God's absence. In other words, the Spirit is the presence of God's promise of himself to us. It is this promise that makes God's absence intolerable to us, and so gives rise to prayer that calls for the coming of God's kingdom, the accomplishment of God's purpose, the hallowing of God's name "on earth as it is in heaven." As the presence of God's promise, the Spirit is the Spirit of Christ, who is, as Paul says, "the yea and amen to all God's promises."

The godlessness and godforsakenness that we express in prayer points to God's coming to us. Insofar as God has come to us, we sing praise; insofar as God is not yet come to us, we pray for his coming. Thus prayer is directed toward praise. Apart from praise (thanks for God's presence), we could not pray (speak of God's absence).

That praise is necessary for prayer is aptly expressed in the liturgical form of the Lord's Prayer. It is generally recognized that the doxology ("for thine is the kingdom and the power and the glory, forever and ever, amen") had no place in the original form of this prayer, but was added for "liturgical" purposes. Despite its "secondary" character, it makes clear the basis of the prayer itself. The ascription of rule, power, and glory to God corresponds to the petitions that begin the prayer. We ask for God's kingdom because "thine is the kingdom"; we ask for God to accomplish his purpose because "thine is the power"; we ask for God to hallow his name because "thine is the glory." We ask for that which is "not yet" because it is "already" here. It is in this sense that we may say that the doxology "belongs to" the Lord's Prayer, even if it had no place in the Prayer's original form.

This unity is expressed in the very form of our public prayer, in which we express praise simply by naming God. The very name "Father" ascribes to God the help and love which we seek. This name is mentioned in the broader context of "Our Father, who art in heaven . . . ," a clause that regularly names the way in which God is, has been, or promises to be present to us. Thus our prayers contain praise—praise that names the basis of our prayer. In this way, too, our prayer depends upon praise.

Despite the reasons for assigning priority to praise over prayer, it is nevertheless true that without prayer praise would be impossible for us, because prayer makes us open to the coming of that which fills our need. If we are unaware of our need, we will not be awake to the coming of that which overcomes it, to the presence of that which we lack. Where there is no prayer, there will be no praise. Apart from prayer, we are oblivious to yearning and so to the joy which overcomes our yearning.

This truth becomes apparent in a variety of ways. The discipline of prayer teaches us to see our life more realistically, and in so doing we learn to distinguish our actual need and deepest yearning from the manufactured needs and bewildered yearnings which are so much a part of our life in a consumer society. Learning this difference also makes it possible for us to distinguish the joy that overwhelms our real need from the titillation that only distracts us. Thus our praise and thanksgiving is freed to become more certain and more joyous. Similarly, prayer teaches us to see our actual situation in the light of God's promise. In this way we are prepared to see our life and that of our world in the light of God's action and presence. Our prayer thus prevents our praise from becoming unrealistic, unworldly, or merely self-indulgent.

As different as prayer and praise are, they belong together. Apart from one, the other would be unintelligible—indeed, impossible. Only in alternation with one another, in this contrast and complementarity, does our turning toward God take on the appropriate directness, boldness, truthfulness, and realism. Only together do prayer and praise reflect their origin and basis in our crucified and resurrected Lord. Only thus do we direct ourselves to God in Jesus' name and for his sake.

B. THE LITURGICAL RHYTHM OF PRAYER AND PRAISE

We express the togetherness of prayer and praise in the rhythm of our common worship. This togetherness is expressed even in the terms we use to describe our worship—"common prayer" and "celebration." The first term obviously emphasizes prayer, and the other emphasizes praise, yet they name the same service. (The term "worship" also designates this activity with the emphasis on praise, as does the term "eucharist.")

The activity we engage in together is not *either* prayer *or* praise, but the two together in succession and alternation. In the liturgy of our common service we do not "split the difference" or take a middle course; we give full expression both to our yearning for God (prayer) and to our joy in God (praise), to our lack and to our fullness, to God's absence and to God's presence, to protest and to celebration. If we see our common worship in this way, we may begin to see how we may shape it in appropriate and helpful ways.

Whether our worship is High-Church or Low-Church, "free" or "liturgical," it is always shaped by some rhythm, some alternation between prayer and praise. Indeed, it is this alternation that gives movement and order to that worship. We can imagine worship without preaching, without sacrament, perhaps even without the "reading" of Scripture. But it is difficult indeed to imagine worship in which prayer and songs of praise have no part, because together these constitute the way in which our words and actions are directed to God. Apart from this direction and orientation, there is no worship.

The order of our worship is the order of prayer and praise. Beginning with the prayer of invocation, prayer and praise succeed one another like breathing in and breathing out, a rhythm that gives life and form to the life of the community before God. The specific character of this order varies widely in the worship of different traditions, but any ordering of worship—even the most experimental celebration—requires attention to this rhythm. A string of songs of praise can result in a feverish and breathless exercise; an unbroken succession of prayers can become self-inflated and self-preoccupied. The absence of praise makes our prayer grim, desperate, or magical; the absence of prayer makes our praise unfocused, unreal, and arbitrary.

A worship service that properly maintains the rhythms of prayer and praise will be one that expresses both the absence and the presence of God, and is thus truthful worship. It will embrace both the actual misery and the ordinary joy of our life, binding them together by directing them to God "in Jesus' name" and "for Jesus' sake." No reform of worship, no "liturgical renewal" can possibly succeed if it does not make our worship more truthful, more bold, more clear, because more firmly anchored in the life and destiny of Jesus.

C. PRAYER AND PRAISE AS THE RHYTHM OF LIFE

We have described two contrasting actions, each of which has its own implications for shaping our lifestyle. Thus our life as a whole may be described as "ceaseless prayer" and as "continuous praise." We have seen both how disparate these actions are, and how intimately they are bound together. What can it mean that our life as a life "in Christ" can and must have such deeply different characteristics?

1. Diversity

That our life has such different charcteristics should provide the clearest possible warning against any attempt to reduce it to a single principle, a uniform structure, something that conforms to an external law. To speak of a lifestyle shaped by prayer and praise is not to speak of a new law to which we are obliged to conform, nor of the slogan of a particular party line within the community of faith. The radical difference between prayer and praise suggests instead a profound diversity of lifestyles, all structured by these activities.

The alternation of prayer and praise corresponds to the alternation in our life and our world between God's absence and presence, between emptiness and fullness, between oppression and liberation. James recognizes something like this alternation and its expression in worship when he writes, "If anyone is in trouble, let him pray. If anyone is happy, let him sing" (Jas. 5:13). Our existence is not made up of prayer or praise alone, but of the meaningful alternation between these two actions.

This freedom and diversity that characterize a lifestyle shaped by prayer and praise is something we may see in still another way. In this discussion we have returned repeatedly to Paul's metaphor of "body," which Paul uses to name our way of being in the world. As such, "body" names our whole way of being involved in the world of other other persons, of society, and of nature. This body of relationships may be a "body of death"—a lifeless involvement with the world, a relationship without power or energy and governed by anxiety, enmity, and fear. Or this body of involvements may be a "body of glory" or a body of worship—a way of life that is in lively solidarity with our neighbor. We will return to this contrast shortly, but first let us notice, again, that the metaphor for our life in the world is "body." Our bodies are as different as are our situations in the world—and just that different are the ways in which our emptiness and fullness are formed and expressed by words and deeds.

The shape of prayer, its underlying structure remains the same despite the immense variation in the concerns we express and the ways we express them. The shape of praise also remains the same, though it is sung in many different tongues and in many different circumstances. The same can be said of a Christian lifestyle shaped like and formed by prayer and praise. Such a lifestyle will vary greatly from person to person because of the different ways in which we are "embodied" in the world, yet this diversity itself has an underlying order and structure corresponding to the shape of prayer and praise.

2. Clarity

A lifestyle governed by prayer does not oppose a lifestyle governed by praise; rather, both stand in opposition to a lifestyle that has become unconscious of both need and fullness, of both pain and joy. They stand in stark contrast to the mindless and unconscious life that never knows its need and is oblivious to deep joy.

We know this mindlessness all too well. We are too familiar with what it means to hide our own yearning and need from ourselves so that we no longer know what it is that we want, so that we are at the mercy of every sort of fabricated need our society has developed. And we know only too well what it is to be so oblivious to need and desire that we force ourselves to be oblivious to the needs and desires of our neighbor. If this were not so, why would we insulate ourselves from our neighbor's need by isolating the diseased, the dying, the old, the poor, the imprisoned, the insane? The structures of oppression depend for their survival upon this blindness, this oblivion, this mindlessness. Without it, our consumer society could not exist.

We also know what it is to be oblivious to joy. We know very well what it is like to "pursue happiness," and to be so engrossed in doing so that we fail to appreciate what we have. Only later, much later, do we "remember the good old days," times we were blind to because of our anxious distraction. And surely we know what it is like to be so caught up with the pursuit of "enough" that another's joy is a cause for envy and suspicion rather than rejoicing. Indeed, how quickly is our own joy displaced by a kind of reflexive envy because we fear losing it, or are trying to figure out how to preserve it? Thus we engage in the colossal stupidity of coveting our own joy. We also know what it is to become so oblivious to the character and experience of joy that we accept the pretended necessity of institutions and structures. If this were not so, we would not feel threatened by other people's revolutions against the system, nor would we know so well what it is to be so mesmerized by necessity that we lose the capacity to laugh at privilege, at power, at death, at ourselves. We have become oblivious to what it is like to be glad.

Paul speaks of "reasonable worship," and this is no careless phrase. For a life shaped by prayer and praise is a life awakened to and aware of itself and its world, a sharp contrast to the irrational, unconscious, and mindless life, which knows neither itself nor its world, which neither knows its own need nor is aware of its own exuberance. The life that is shaped by prayer and praise is awake and aware, and thus "rational" or "reasonable." Our bodies—that is, our lifestyle and our involvement in the world—are presented as a reasonable worship when they are formed by and shaped like prayer and praise. When they are not so shaped, they become like a "body of death," distracted by anxiety and fear, oblivious and mindless.

3. Forming a Lifestyle

a. Individuality and Community

Our lives are to be shaped as a reasonable worship. We have already seen that this does not mean that our lives then conform to a single rule or principle; rather, the rhythm or "beat" of prayer and praise not only permits but provokes diversity and individuality of expression—just as the beat of music permits considerable variation in the steps of the dancers who, despite all idiosyncracies of individual movement, dance with the same rhythm and therefore with one another.

Our lives, too, have rhythms that unite us. We each form or develop our own style of dancing, our own style of responding to God's presence or absence, to the pain and joy of our neighbor, to the oppression and liberation of the poor.

What joins us together is the rhythm to which we move, the beat that orders our life—the rhythm of prayer and praise.

Too often we think of a Christian lifestyle as though it meant marching in lockstep—all of us wearing the same uniform and the same expression, all doing the same thing. But this grim goose-stepping of moralism is the march of death, not the dance of life. It insists that everyone perform the same act, use the same language, abstain from the same vices, get involved in the same way. The moralism of the right would have everyone omit wine from their diets and substitute a pious vocabulary for "colorful language." The moralism of the left would have us all carry the same signs and march in the same demonstrations. The moralism of the center would have us all go to church and Sunday school, all produce 1.3 children, all be good citizens. Each in its own way would prescribe not only the beat but the music, not only the music but the dance, not only the dance but the costume for our lifestyle. Fortunately, these moralisms—deadly when they stand alone—exist side by side. Together, despite themselves, they almost manage to dance. The Spirit is not easily resisted—not even by the Church.

In forming a lifestyle, we are not reduced to the choice between competing moralisms—we are invited to "dance," to learn to present our own bodies as a reasonable worship. This means taking a fresh look at our lives, our relationships, our involvements, and asking in what ways they may more clearly attest to the underlying beat of prayer and praise. In answering this question we may form an alternation between play and protest, between fasting and feasting, between sighing and singing. For each of us this style may be different, reflecting the difference in our bodies, our relationships, our discernments. Some will choose to eat while others fast; some may protest an injustice while others celebrate a liberation. Here there is no automatic conformity, though there may be spontaneous community. For the Spirit who gives many gifts and assigns many tasks is the same Spirit who calls us to life and invites us to the dance.

I know that many of us will find this degree of freedom and responsibility uncomfortable. We wish to know more clearly what is "the right thing to do"; we take comfort in the more clear-cut togetherness of a common model. If we must dance, we would prefer the classic sameness of the waltz to the seeming anarchy of modern dance. We would rather take the chance of being moralists than the risk of spontaneous freedom. And taking this position is permissible—so long as we do not cut ourselves off from all those who make different choices, who imitate different patterns or seek their own style.

Saint Paul refers to the Church as a whole as "the body of Christ," a body composed of many members, a unity of many bodies. It is one by virtue of the Spirit, who gives it life; by virtue of Jesus, who is its unifying head; by virtue of the Father of Jesus, to whom it is directed. Yet it is also many by virtue of the multiplicity of styles within it; indeed, this multiplicity is as essential as the unity. It is precisely as the community of Jesus that this body is composed of charismatics and civic-minded, revolutionaries and monks, the pious and the decidedly impious. Taken by itself, each lifestyle is lacking. Only together, without envy and arrogance, do these become the body of Christ.

Whether we choose our own way or adapt ourselves to some already proven way, we need this diversity. Otherwise there is no dance, and no body of Christ. It is because of the strength of those groups that would form the multi-faceted dance of life into a grim march (to the left, to the right, or in the center) that I have felt it necessary to stress the freedom and responsibility involved in discovering our own style.

Just as those who choose to imitate a pattern of life need to beware of absolutizing this pattern, so those who reject such patterns (as moralistic conformity) must beware of an anarchy which only succeeds in becoming unfree. No bondage is more restrictive than that which ties me to a whim and to the moment. In escaping the bondage of moralism, I may only succumb to the tyranny of anarchic mood and arbitrary whim.

When we embark upon the path of forming, in freedom and responsibility, our own lifestyle, the question of form and rhythm becomes all the more urgent. Here, where religion and piety are most in decline, stands the greatest need for liturgy. Here, where conformity is least possible, stands our greatest need for community. For in the improvisation of a dance we need most to hear the rhythm, a beat sounded loudly and firmly. For here if we miss the beat or lose the rhythm, we cannot fall back on imitation, and there is no net to break our fall. Thus the more "worldly" and "liberated" our lifestyle as Christians, the more we may need and welcome the clarity of corporate prayer and praise.

b. Worship and Life

Nothing could be worse than the separation of worship and life, a separation that can produce a variety of aberrations. It may produce a merely formal and aesthetic liturgy that is performed perfunctorily in a kind of liturgical museum or it may produce a worship "experience" that serves primarily as an emotional release of tensions. In both cases worship has become a separate act—merely decorative or cathartic—that is cut off from life in the world. It is precisely when worship is thus separated from everyday life that it is most readily replaced. The "beautiful" worship service is readily replaced by the Sunday afternoon concert; the "enthusiastic" worship service is readily replaced by the pep rally and the weekend football game. Ironically, the more "religious" (separated) our worship, the more easily it is replaced by the "secular."

But these aberrations in worship also produce aberrations in life; they make our everyday life formless, without identity. This formlessness occurs whether we "worship" or not. That is, the regular practice of a worship that has no meaning for our everyday existence leaves that life basically unchanged, though it may be "punctuated" by pious phrases and religious practices. The rejection of such an unworldly piety and religiosity in favor of life in the world—even when done in the name of Christian freedom—also leaves life without form, order, or rhythm. Such form as our life has in such circumstances is arbitrary and capricious, ruled by the whims or pressures of the moment.

The proper function of worship is to form our life in the world as an existence "before God." [1]

[1]This has important implications for the way in which we form our worship, or "renew" our liturgies. Many attempt to improve the worship of our communities by imposing aesthetic or historical criteria upon this worship. All too often this is what is meant by attempting to become "more

D. THE RHYTHM OF LOVE

In the togetherness of prayer and praise we may discern the twin aspects of love: desire and delight. These correspond to the absence and the presence, the need and the gift, of the other. As a life of love, our existence is suspended between desire and delight.

Our life with our neighbor is clearly compounded of desire and delight. We need the other in order to be. We cannot live alone without touch, without affection, without help, and so we desire the other. This desire may turn upon itself and our neighbor—it may consume and violate, imprison and destroy. But even in its corruption it is a cry for the other, a longing for the presence of love and joy even when it banishes both. Yet even in this history of betrayal and longing, we anticipate the end of desire in delight. We know this in moments of joy and gratitude, in moments when desire is transfigured by delight. Without such moments of anticipated and actual delight, how should we continue to desire? These are the moments when the other is to us neither an ally nor an enemy but a fitting help (Gen. 2:18) and a neighbor (Luke 10:36-7).

Our life with God follows a similar pattern. It is more often one of desire than of delight, of longing than of joy, of enduring than of enjoyment, of the absence than of the reign of God. The life of faith is mostly one of longing, of waiting, of hoping for that which is not present, not evident and so unseen. Whenever we seek to possess that for which we hope, we lapse into idolatry and superstition—and so into religion. Yet even in the corruption of faith and hope, even in this degradation and betrayal of our desire for God, we may discern our anticipation of the end of desire in delight. This, too, we

---

liturgical." But this only makes our worship more precious, arcane, and irrelevant. Others, often under the banner of "celebration," attempt to make our worship more expressive of the experience and "feeling" of a particular congregation. But worship conceived in this way becomes as formless as the life it "expresses." Both liturgical movements and celebration movements have important contributions to make. The first stresses the historical continuity of the life of the community; the second the enlivening effect of the Spirit—both correctly see the danger of a dispirited and perfunctory worship. But both likewise fail to grasp the essential character of worship. For our worship of prayer and praise misses its goal if it does not succeed in shaping our life in the world.

know in moments of joy and gratitude; without such moments, how should we continue to desire? These are the moments when we recognize Emmanuel even in the cry of the godforsaken and are empowered by the Spirit to confidently call "Abba" in surprise and joy.

In our life with the other and in the world, we know far more of desire than of delight, of need than of fullness. Yet delight is more important than desire; it is the goal already claimed by desire.

Prayer and praise follow this same pattern. We wait and yearn and therefore pray for that time when our prayer will be transfigured into praise. We sing praise when our prayer is, however fleetingly, punctuated by the presence of that for which we long. Since this presence has been both promised and made flesh in Jesus, we conclude our prayer and begin our song "in Jesus' name."